BARsecrets

California Community Property

Substantive Law and Model Essays

Dennis P. Saccuzzo

Nancy E. Johnson

Applications of Psychology to Law, Inc.
San Diego, California

Other books in the Bar Secrets® series:

An Essay Approach for the Multistate Subjects
An Essay Approach for the California-Specific Subjects
Federal Civil Procedure
Remedies
California Wills & Trusts
Professional Responsibility - ABA Rules plus California Distinctions
Corporations - Federal Securities and the Common Law

Hidden Issues – Beating the Bar at its own Game
The Multistate Subjects
The California-Specific Subjects
Model Approach to Applying the Law
The Essay Workbook
The 1L Book
The 2L Book

APL
Applications of Psychology to Law

FIRST EDITION (SECOND PRINTING), 2006.
Copyright © 2005 by Applications of Psychology to Law, Inc.

ISBN 1-933089-07-5

For further information, please contact *Applications of Psychology to Law, Inc.*
2341 Jefferson Street, Suite 101
San Diego, CA 92110 – 3009

http://www.barsecrects.com

Telephone: 619.299.8525
FAX: 619.299.8527
E-mail: info@barsecrets.com

Contents

About Us

Bar Secrets® is an integrated program of materials developed by Applications of Psychology to Law, Inc., a corporation founded to assist law students and attorneys to understand principles of psychology as they apply to law practice. It was founded by 2 members of the California Bar who are each also licensed California psychologists. We are located in San Diego, California. Our website for Bar Secrets is located at www.barsecrets.com.

We developed the Bar Secrets® instructional materials in order to make the job of assimilating the law and writing law essays easier, more efficient, and less stressful. We do that by applying the latest knowledge from psychology -- human memory, cognition, and neuropsychology -- to the problem of organizing, learning, and retaining in active memory the huge number of rules and principles that form the law.

Dennis P. Saccuzzo is a professor and attorney. He holds a Ph.D. in clinical psychology and a J.D. degree. He has lectured extensively on the application of psychology to the study of law, including problems of human learning, memory, personality, stress, and the schematic approach to studying any complex subject. He has authored or co-authored over 300 professional publications and papers, including 27 books. Currently he is a Professor of Psychology at San Diego State University and an adjunct professor at California Western School of Law. His California psychologist license number is PSY 4606.

Nancy E. Johnson is a California licensed psychologist (PSY 13706) and attorney who holds a Ph.D. in clinical psychology and a J.D. degree. She has lectured extensively on the application of psychology to the study of law, including problems of human learning and memory from a neuropsychological perspective. She has authored or co-authored over 150 professional publications and papers, including 19 books. Currently she is an adjunct professor at California Western School of Law.

Preface

This book contains previously unpublished material as well as excerpts from the following books:

Bar Secrets: The California-Specific Subjects

Bar Secrets: The Essay Workbook

Bar Secrets: Model Approach to Applying the Law

Bar Secrets: An Essay Approach for the California-Specific Subjects

All of these books are published by Applications of Psychology to Law, Inc., a corporation devoted to applying the field of psychology to the field of law. One major issue, mastering the vast amount of knowledge necessary to pass Bar examinations, is addressed in the Bar Secrets® bundle of substantive law and essay writing books. For more information on these books, visit our website at www.barsecrets.com.

Our Approach to Writing

Our approach to essay writing is straightforward, effective, and easy to learn. We begin with a very brief statement of the issue. Next, we discuss the relevant background law as extracted from the Bar Secrets® schematic outline/flow charts such as the community property outline in this book. An outline contains the basic skeleton of the law, including definitions, rules, elements, factors, standards, and other important information. A flow chart is like a diagram or map. It illustrates the essential steps or basic decisions one might make in responding to an essay fact pattern. We combine them by integrating flow charts into the outline, making the law more accessible than any other possible format.

These outlines/flow charts have many advantages. At a glance, they present the overall organization of the law and provide a tool into which you can integrate new knowledge. They function as excellent issue checklists to aid in spotting all issues raised by a fact pattern. They can also be used in the encoding (i.e., learning) and retrieval (i.e., recall) process.

Background Law. From the background law comes the premise from which you begin your discussion of any issue. You should note the difference between presenting background law and the approach in a simple IRAC (Issue, Rule, Analysis, Conclusion). In an IRAC format, one presents only the on-point rule of law, a tight-fitting premise from which to reason deductively based on the facts. The IRAC format, taught widely, gives the minimum law needed to analyze an issue. In our experience, the IRAC approach, even when all the issues are covered, is not well received by Bar examiners and most law professors.

In providing background law, we give more than the minimum on-point rule. Instead, we try to provide a broader context including any relevant standards, definitions, and factors where appropriate.

A _definition_ tells what a term means. Generally, all legal terms of art should be defined. At a minimum, in California community property one must define community property (CP) and separate property (SP).

A _presumption_ is an assumption that will be held as true unless it can be successfully rebutted by its opponent. For example, under California community property laws it is presumed that all property acquired during the marriage by the skill and effort of either spouse is CP. Unless the opponent of the presumption can produce sufficient evidence to the contrary, the court will assume that the presumption is true.

Elements are the specifics that must be proven to make a prima facie case. For example, the two elements of a valid premarital agreement are (1) signed and (2) writing. Issues are triggered when there are facts that go to an element. Where there are elements, all must be established to succeed in proving one's case. For example, to prove that a premarital agreement is valid, it is necessary to establish both elements. If only one of the two elements can be established, the agreement will not be valid.

Where all of the elements can be met, it still may be possible to avoid the full effects if an _exception_ can be found. Exceptions are the specific circumstances under which a court will override a general rule. For example, there are 4 exceptions to a premarital agreement: (1) full performance, (2) estoppel, (3) violations of public policy, and (4) undue influence. The first two exceptions would allow enforcement of a premarital agreement even if all the elements cannot be met. The second two would invalidate the agreement even if all the elements can be met. Where there are exceptions, it is necessary to address each to see if they would apply in any given fact pattern to modify the general rule.

The Analysis. After presenting the background law, we skip a line (for good form and ease of reading) and give our analysis. A good analysis uses as many relevant facts as possible to argue a point. In basic terms, you must _prove your case_.

A common mistake is to be _conclusory_. A conclusory analysis begins with the law and then asserts, without proof or facts, that the case has been made. For example, one might give the rule that quasi-community property (QCP) is property acquired by a married couple in another jurisdiction that would have been CP if the acquiring spouse was domiciled in California, followed by the conclusion that "here, we have QCP." You must use facts to argue that the property indeed qualifies as QCP by showing that it would have been CP if acquired in California. This is proving your case. Competent attorneys do not go into the courtroom and simply announce their conclusions. Instead, they establish facts and then use those facts to prove their case.

In conducting your analysis, it is usually better to take a position and support it with facts and legal principles than to "ping pong" by arguing both sides. The vast majority of issues are clear one way or another. Coming up with strained counter arguments in such circumstances is counterproductive because it wastes time. It is only where an issue is arguable or unclear that both sides should be given. Even here, you must be decisive and come down on one side or the other.

An idealized or model approach to analysis would be to begin with the facts that go to your conclusion or element, state the relevant conclusion, then reinforce your analysis by adding a "because" clause. For example, "The house was acquired using earnings acquired during the existence of the marriage **[facts]**, therefore it is CP **[conclusion]** _because_ all property acquired during the marriage by the skill and effort of either spouse is presumed CP **["because" clause]**."

Conclude with confidence. It is essential to articulate your conclusion, and with some confidence. We have observed selected answers from successful candidates on the California Bar's website that are just plain wrong, but which are asserted with such confidence as to be convincing. By contrast, candidates who fail to conclude, or show uncertainty are usually penalized with low scores.

Each of our models presents clear illustrations of our suggested writing format. In consequence, the approach is illustrated repeatedly, making it easy to learn and adapt to your own personal style. Please note, however, that at times we deviate from the idealized approach to illustrate the various strategies for finishing under time constraints.

Strategies for Finishing

Needless to say, it is important to finish. Because of time constraints, it is not always possible or even desirable to routinely and mechanically follow the idealized approach. Instead, there are a number of good strategies that can be used in the middle of an answer to vary your style and finish.

*First, you must realize the importance of **primacy effects**, or first impressions. Graders make up their minds quickly, and once made up, find it difficult to change. An answer that begins strongly, according to the suggested (idealized) format with good, accurate background law, a strong analysis that uses the relevant facts to prove or disprove a point, and a confident conclusion is well on the way to a high score.*

In the middle it is necessary to find a way to speed things up, because generally one should raise all colorable issues (i.e., where some fact goes to at least one element of a prima facie case) unless expressly excluded by the instructions in the fact pattern. This can be done in a number of ways. One is to enumerate the rule and elements, but rather than discuss each element, just go to the one that fails to show a particular case can be made. A second approach is to discuss the facts and merely imply, rather than articulate, the relevant law. There is even room for an occasional conclusory response for minor issues. Each of these approaches is illustrated in the models included in this book. You should try to note when they are used to get a better idea how to use these strategies to cover your bases in terms of issue-spotting, and also finish the essay.

The Schematic Approach

No one – not even a chess master – can learn the thousands of rules and elements that appear on the Bar exam without a method. The schematic approach provides such a method by showing you the most effective way of organizing and learning. It is faster, more efficient and much easier than conventional methods.

In the schematic approach, information is presented the way the human brain stores it. In learning any topic, the brain begins by forming a simple general categorical framework, for which the Swiss scientist Piaget coined the word "schemata." Detailed information is then added to that framework in stages.

As illustrated in this book, Bar Secrets® substantive law books provide schematic overviews for each subject. These schematic overviews begin with the simplest, broadest categorization of the law. Community property has 5: basic definitions, legal presumptions and rules, central issues, involvement of third parties, and distribution of assets. These 5 broad categories are referred to as level one.

Following the level one outline, there is a second outline that again lists each of the major broad categories. Each broad category is then connected to two or more major issues. This outline is referred to as level two. Level two contains all of the major issues that you'll be expected to spot. You must have each of these issues at your fingertips. For example, level 2 of involvement of third parties consists of spouse management and control, creditors, and third party transfers.

Following levels one and two are the details, definitions, and major rules of law associated with each of the basic issues. These details are referred to as level three. It is necessary for you to have a recall knowledge of each of the rules of law, definitions, standards, elements, factors, and tests (if any) contained in level three. You must also know, and be able to communicate, the effect of any rule of law. To develop such a recall knowledge, we recommend that you study the rule, definition, standard, etc. and attempt to write it down from memory. Keep checking yourself until you can write it out perfectly.

Our approach to law studies is based on scientific principles in cognitive psychology and neuropsychology that we have been using and teaching for a number of years. In brief, we present the information in a hierarchical schematic format that follows the natural way information is organized by the human brain. A schematic represents the structure of an organized body of knowledge. Once a person has the basic structure, it is easy to learn and remember the details, which is why law professors have little difficulty picking up and remembering small details of law quickly and with little effort.

Secrets of Human Memory

Studying for law exams or the Bar exam doesn't have to be torture. You don't have to memorize hundreds of disjointed rules and elements. This is not the smart way to use your memory.

What is memory? Well, it's many things. People who claim to have poor memories really mean they have poor "retrieval" skills. Retrieval means recalling, or recovering information once learned. One of the most important secrets of memory is that one's ability to retrieve (recall) information depends on how we deal with it in the first place!

The term "encoding" refers to getting information into memory and transforming it into a form that can be used. The secret to memory is that the way you encode (that is, put information into memory) determines your ability to retrieve it when you need it. By making your encoding more effective, you can greatly enhance your recall without using any more time.

There are numerous ways to make encoding more efficient. In a nutshell, we remember those things that we think about and that we relate to our broader structure of knowledge. For example, when students were divided into 2 groups and given different memorization strategies, they had markedly different rates of success. The rote approach (repeatedly reading and repeating information – the approach most students take) took almost twice as long and resulted in roughly half the retention of the active approach. You too can improve your memory by following an active approach:

1. Attend to the meaning of what you're studying.
2. Form images to help you remember.
3. Consciously encourage yourself to be alert and attend carefully.
4. Without notes, practice recalling what you studied in order to consolidate it.

Other effective techniques of encoding use the schematic approach advocated in Bar Secrets® and involve imposing an organization on the material. It turns out that imposing any organization is better than none at all. To improve you encoding, begin by memorizing Level 1 of your schematic outline. Then read the main body with the goal of understanding everything well enough to explain the concepts in a study group and answer any questions about them. Finally, memorize Level 2. Practice recalling Levels 1 and 2, as well as any definitions, rules, standards, elements, or factors.

COMMUNITY PROPERTY

LEVEL 1

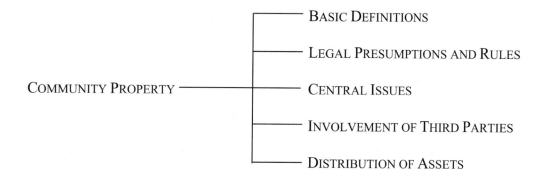

COMMUNITY PROPERTY

- BASIC DEFINITIONS
- LEGAL PRESUMPTIONS AND RULES
- CENTRAL ISSUES
- INVOLVEMENT OF THIRD PARTIES
- DISTRIBUTION OF ASSETS

[THIS PAGE INTENTIONALLY LEFT BLANK.]

COMMUNITY PROPERTY

LEVEL 2

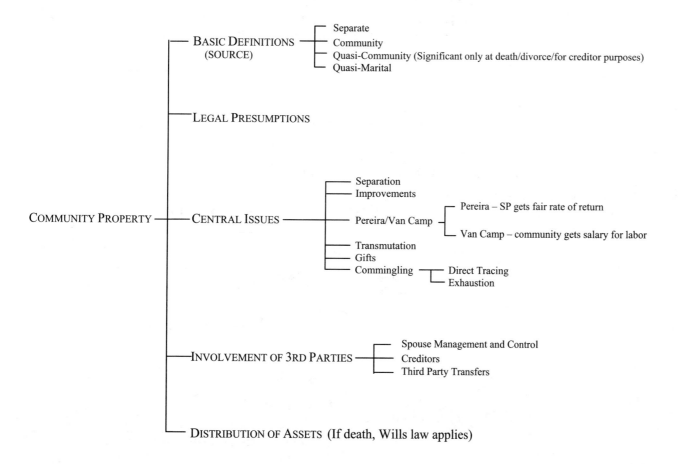

COMMUNITY PROPERTY ———

- BASIC DEFINITIONS (SOURCE)
  - Separate
  - Community
  - Quasi-Community (Significant only at death/divorce/for creditor purposes)
  - Quasi-Marital

- LEGAL PRESUMPTIONS

- CENTRAL ISSUES
  - Separation
  - Improvements
  - Pereira/Van Camp
    - Pereira – SP gets fair rate of return
    - Van Camp – community gets salary for labor
  - Transmutation
  - Gifts
  - Commingling
    - Direct Tracing
    - Exhaustion

- INVOLVEMENT OF 3RD PARTIES
  - Spouse Management and Control
  - Creditors
  - Third Party Transfers

- DISTRIBUTION OF ASSETS (If death, Wills law applies)

COMMUNITY PROPERTY – ISSUE COVERAGE ON THE CALIFORNIA BAR EXAM

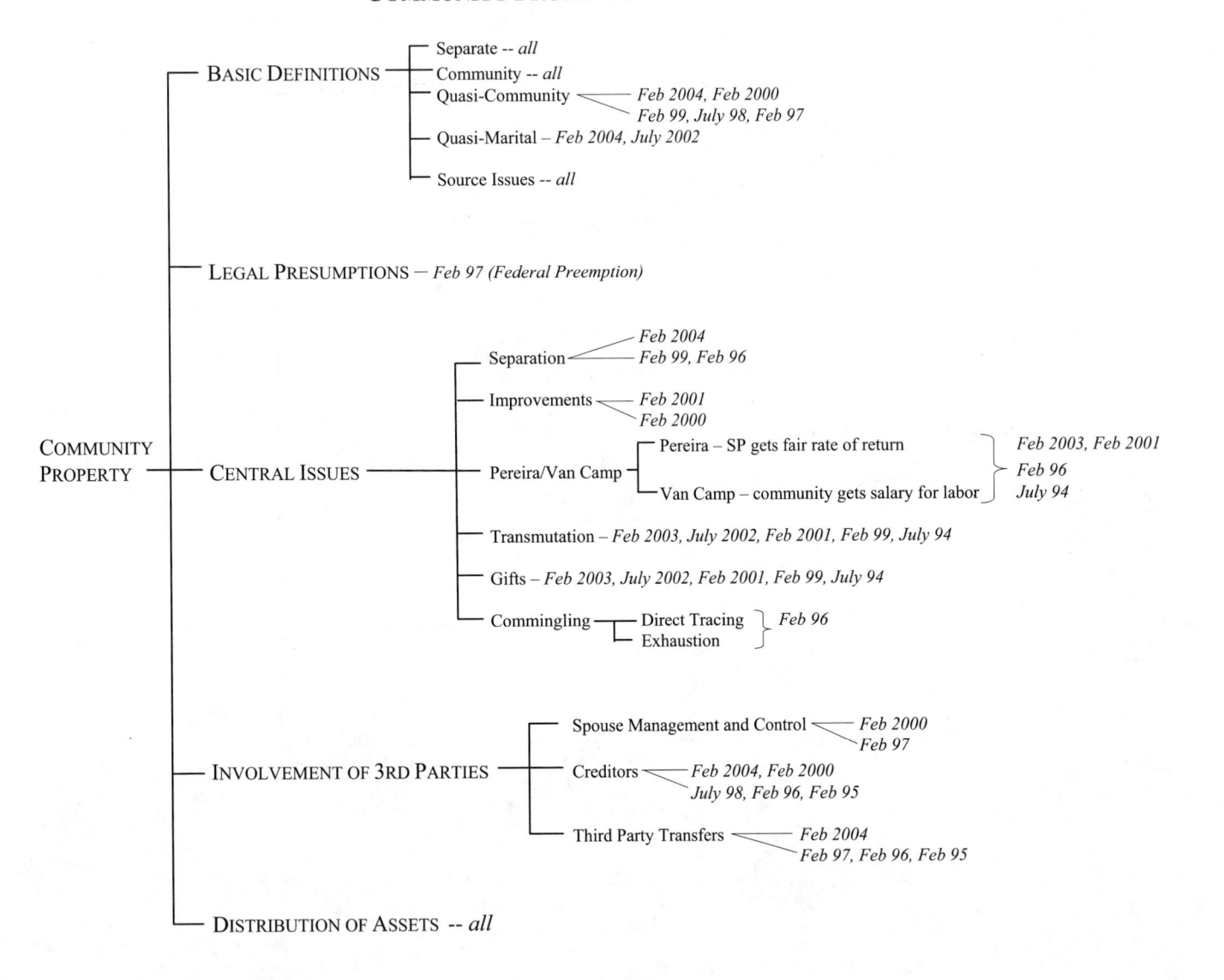

COMMUNITY PROPERTY

- **BASIC DEFINITIONS**
  - Separate -- *all*
  - Community -- *all*
  - Quasi-Community — *Feb 2004, Feb 2000, Feb 99, July 98, Feb 97*
  - Quasi-Marital – *Feb 2004, July 2002*
  - Source Issues -- *all*

- **LEGAL PRESUMPTIONS** — *Feb 97 (Federal Preemption)*

- **CENTRAL ISSUES**
  - Separation — *Feb 2004, Feb 99, Feb 96*
  - Improvements — *Feb 2001, Feb 2000*
  - Pereira/Van Camp
    - Pereira – SP gets fair rate of return — *Feb 2003, Feb 2001, Feb 96, July 94*
    - Van Camp – community gets salary for labor
  - Transmutation – *Feb 2003, July 2002, Feb 2001, Feb 99, July 94*
  - Gifts – *Feb 2003, July 2002, Feb 2001, Feb 99, July 94*
  - Commingling
    - Direct Tracing — *Feb 96*
    - Exhaustion

- **INVOLVEMENT OF 3RD PARTIES**
  - Spouse Management and Control — *Feb 2000, Feb 97*
  - Creditors — *Feb 2004, Feb 2000, July 98, Feb 96, Feb 95*
  - Third Party Transfers — *Feb 2004, Feb 97, Feb 96, Feb 95*

- **DISTRIBUTION OF ASSETS** -- *all*

I. BASIC DEFINITIONS

LEVEL 3

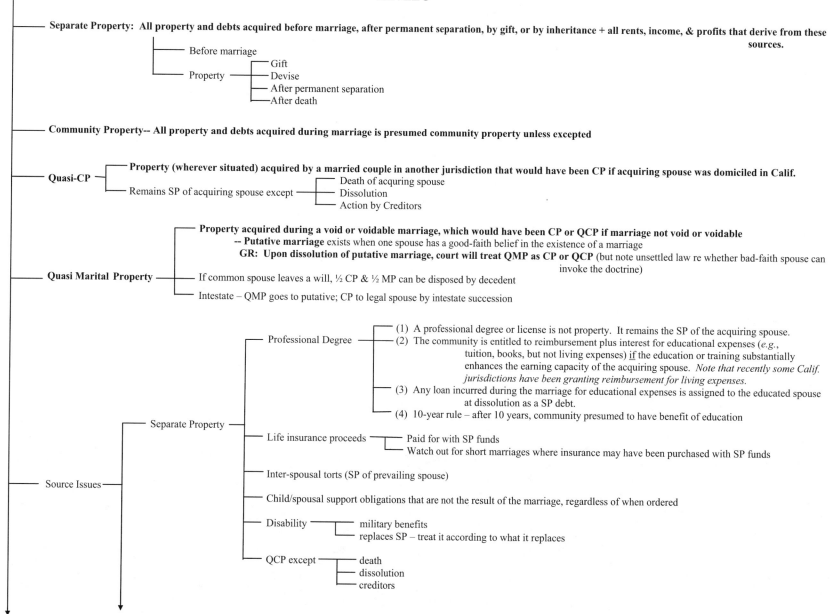

Separate Property: **All property and debts acquired before marriage, after permanent separation, by gift, or by inheritance + all rents, income, & profits that derive from these sources.**

- Before marriage
- Property
  - Gift
  - Devise
  - After permanent separation
  - After death

Community Property-- **All property and debts acquired during marriage is presumed community property unless excepted**

Quasi-CP
- **Property (wherever situated) acquired by a married couple in another jurisdiction that would have been CP if acquiring spouse was domiciled in Calif.**
- Remains SP of acquiring spouse except
  - Death of acquiring spouse
  - Dissolution
  - Action by Creditors

Quasi Marital Property
- **Property acquired during a void or voidable marriage, which would have been CP or QCP if marriage not void or voidable**
  -- Putative marriage exists when one spouse has a good-faith belief in the existence of a marriage
  GR: Upon dissolution of putative marriage, court will treat QMP as CP or QCP (but note unsettled law re whether bad-faith spouse can invoke the doctrine)
- If common spouse leaves a will, ½ CP & ½ MP can be disposed by decedent
- Intestate – QMP goes to putative; CP to legal spouse by intestate succession

Source Issues
- Separate Property
  - Professional Degree
    - (1) A professional degree or license is not property. It remains the SP of the acquiring spouse.
    - (2) The community is entitled to reimbursement plus interest for educational expenses (*e.g.*, tuition, books, but not living expenses) <u>if</u> the education or training substantially enhances the earning capacity of the acquiring spouse. *Note that recently some Calif. jurisdictions have been granting reimbursement for living expenses.*
    - (3) Any loan incurred during the marriage for educational expenses is assigned to the educated spouse at dissolution as a SP debt.
    - (4) 10-year rule – after 10 years, community presumed to have benefit of education
  - Life insurance proceeds
    - Paid for with SP funds
    - Watch out for short marriages where insurance may have been purchased with SP funds
  - Inter-spousal torts (SP of prevailing spouse)
  - Child/spousal support obligations that are not the result of the marriage, regardless of when ordered
  - Disability
    - military benefits
    - replaces SP – treat it according to what it replaces
  - QCP except
    - death
    - dissolution
    - creditors

[THIS PAGE INTENTIONALLY LEFT BLANK.]

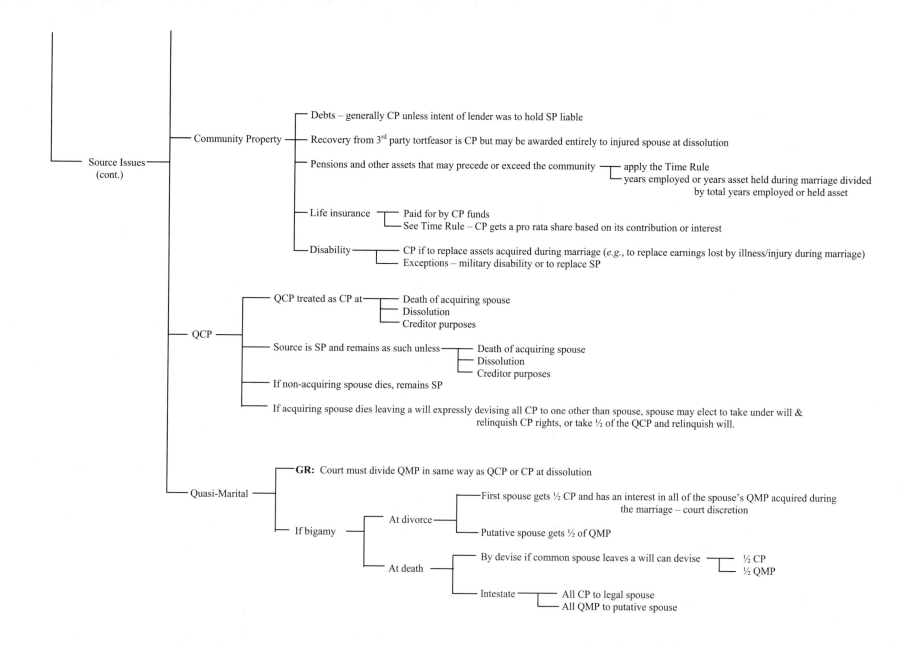

Source Issues (cont.)

Community Property
- Debts – generally CP unless intent of lender was to hold SP liable
- Recovery from 3rd party tortfeasor is CP but may be awarded entirely to injured spouse at dissolution
- Pensions and other assets that may precede or exceed the community
  - apply the Time Rule
  - years employed or years asset held during marriage divided by total years employed or held asset
- Life insurance
  - Paid for by CP funds
  - See Time Rule – CP gets a pro rata share based on its contribution or interest
- Disability
  - CP if to replace assets acquired during marriage (e.g., to replace earnings lost by illness/injury during marriage)
  - Exceptions – military disability or to replace SP

QCP
- QCP treated as CP at
  - Death of acquiring spouse
  - Dissolution
  - Creditor purposes
- Source is SP and remains as such unless
  - Death of acquiring spouse
  - Dissolution
  - Creditor purposes
- If non-acquiring spouse dies, remains SP
- If acquiring spouse dies leaving a will expressly devising all CP to one other than spouse, spouse may elect to take under will & relinquish CP rights, or take ½ of the QCP and relinquish will.

Quasi-Marital
- **GR:** Court must divide QMP in same way as QCP or CP at dissolution
- If bigamy
  - At divorce
    - First spouse gets ½ CP and has an interest in all of the spouse's QMP acquired during the marriage – court discretion
    - Putative spouse gets ½ of QMP
  - At death
    - By devise if common spouse leaves a will can devise
      - ½ CP
      - ½ QMP
    - Intestate
      - All CP to legal spouse
      - All QMP to putative spouse

[THIS PAGE INTENTIONALLY LEFT BLANK.]

II. PRESUMPTIONS

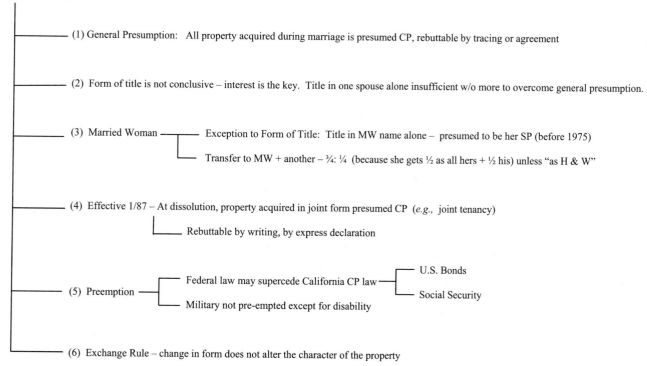

(1) General Presumption: All property acquired during marriage is presumed CP, rebuttable by tracing or agreement

(2) Form of title is not conclusive – interest is the key. Title in one spouse alone insufficient w/o more to overcome general presumption.

(3) Married Woman ⎯ Exception to Form of Title: Title in MW name alone – presumed to be her SP (before 1975)

Transfer to MW + another – ¾: ¼ (because she gets ½ as all hers + ½ his) unless "as H & W"

(4) Effective 1/87 – At dissolution, property acquired in joint form presumed CP (*e.g.,* joint tenancy)

Rebuttable by writing, by express declaration

(5) Preemption ⎯ Federal law may supercede California CP law ⎯ U.S. Bonds

Social Security

Military not pre-empted except for disability

(6) Exchange Rule – change in form does not alter the character of the property

[THIS PAGE INTENTIONALLY LEFT BLANK.]

II. CENTRAL ISSUES

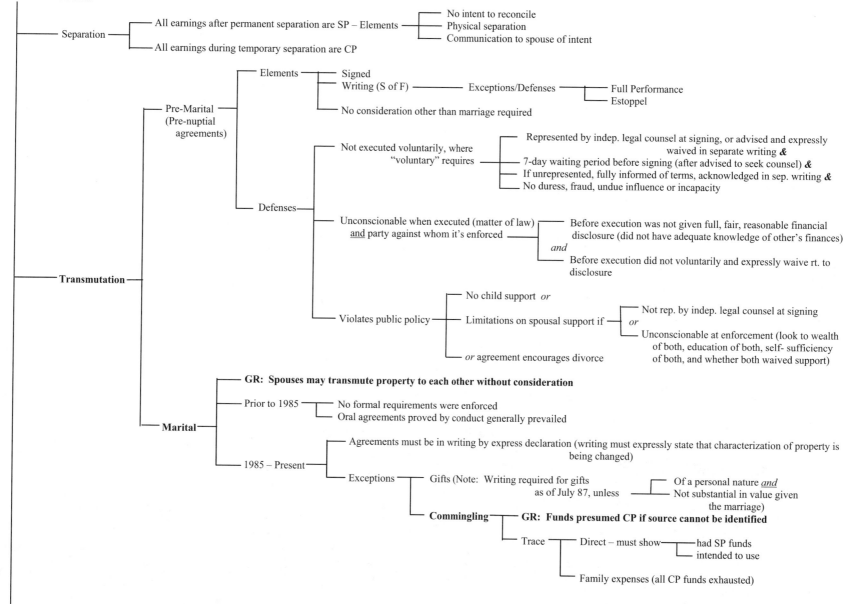

Separation
- All earnings after permanent separation are SP – Elements
  - No intent to reconcile
  - Physical separation
  - Communication to spouse of intent
- All earnings during temporary separation are CP

Transmutation
- **Pre-Marital (Pre-nuptial agreements)**
  - Elements
    - Signed
    - Writing (S of F) — Exceptions/Defenses
      - Full Performance
      - Estoppel
    - No consideration other than marriage required
  - Defenses
    - Not executed voluntarily, where "voluntary" requires
      - Represented by indep. legal counsel at signing, or advised and expressly waived in separate writing **&**
      - 7-day waiting period before signing (after advised to seek counsel) **&**
      - If unrepresented, fully informed of terms, acknowledged in sep. writing **&**
      - No duress, fraud, undue influence or incapacity
    - Unconscionable when executed (matter of law) <u>and</u> party against whom it's enforced
      - Before execution was not given full, fair, reasonable financial disclosure (did not have adequate knowledge of other's finances) *and*
      - Before execution did not voluntarily and expressly waive rt. to disclosure
    - Violates public policy
      - No child support *or*
      - Limitations on spousal support if
        - Not rep. by indep. legal counsel at signing *or*
        - Unconscionable at enforcement (look to wealth of both, education of both, self-sufficiency of both, and whether both waived support)
      - *or* agreement encourages divorce
- **Marital**
  - **GR: Spouses may transmute property to each other without consideration**
  - Prior to 1985
    - No formal requirements were enforced
    - Oral agreements proved by conduct generally prevailed
  - 1985 – Present
    - Agreements must be in writing by express declaration (writing must expressly state that characterization of property is being changed)
    - Exceptions
      - Gifts (Note: Writing required for gifts as of July 87, unless
        - Of a personal nature <u>and</u>
        - Not substantial in value given the marriage)
      - **Commingling**
        - **GR: Funds presumed CP if source cannot be identified**
        - Trace
          - Direct – must show
            - had SP funds
            - intended to use
          - Family expenses (all CP funds exhausted)

[THIS PAGE INTENTIONALLY LEFT BLANK.]

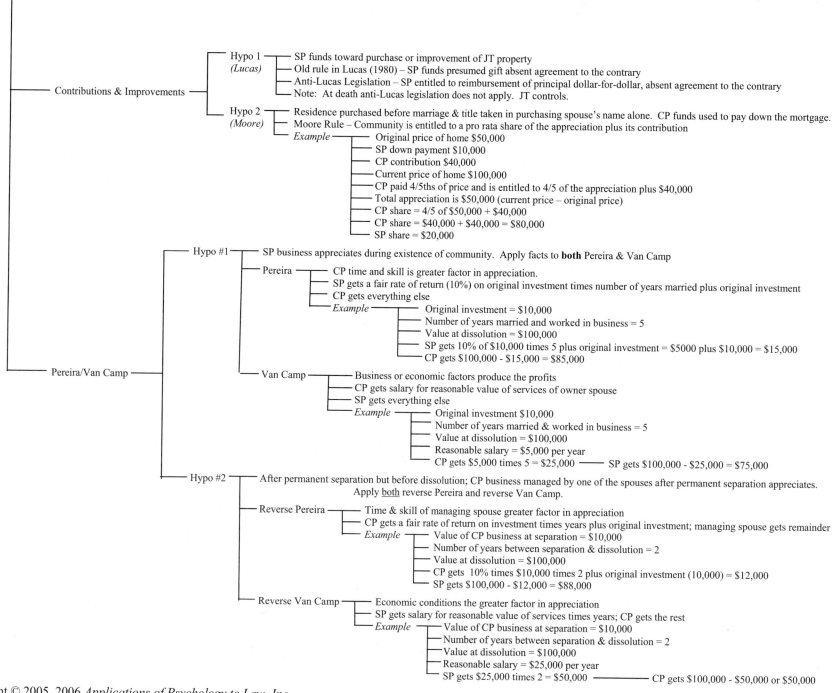

Contributions & Improvements

Hypo 1 (Lucas)
- SP funds toward purchase or improvement of JT property
- Old rule in Lucas (1980) – SP funds presumed gift absent agreement to the contrary
- Anti-Lucas Legislation – SP entitled to reimbursement of principal dollar-for-dollar, absent agreement to the contrary
- Note: At death anti-Lucas legislation does not apply. JT controls.

Hypo 2 (Moore)
- Residence purchased before marriage & title taken in purchasing spouse's name alone. CP funds used to pay down the mortgage.
- Moore Rule – Community is entitled to a pro rata share of the appreciation plus its contribution
- *Example*
  - Original price of home $50,000
  - SP down payment $10,000
  - CP contribution $40,000
  - Current price of home $100,000
  - CP paid 4/5ths of price and is entitled to 4/5 of the appreciation plus $40,000
  - Total appreciation is $50,000 (current price – original price)
  - CP share = 4/5 of $50,000 + $40,000
  - CP share = $40,000 + $40,000 = $80,000
  - SP share = $20,000

Pereira/Van Camp

Hypo #1 — SP business appreciates during existence of community. Apply facts to **both** Pereira & Van Camp

Pereira
- CP time and skill is greater factor in appreciation.
- SP gets a fair rate of return (10%) on original investment times number of years married plus original investment
- CP gets everything else
- *Example*
  - Original investment = $10,000
  - Number of years married and worked in business = 5
  - Value at dissolution = $100,000
  - SP gets 10% of $10,000 times 5 plus original investment = $5000 plus $10,000 = $15,000
  - CP gets $100,000 - $15,000 = $85,000

Van Camp
- Business or economic factors produce the profits
- CP gets salary for reasonable value of services of owner spouse
- SP gets everything else
- *Example*
  - Original investment $10,000
  - Number of years married & worked in business = 5
  - Value at dissolution = $100,000
  - Reasonable salary = $5,000 per year
  - CP gets $5,000 times 5 = $25,000 ——— SP gets $100,000 - $25,000 = $75,000

Hypo #2 — After permanent separation but before dissolution; CP business managed by one of the spouses after permanent separation appreciates. Apply <u>both</u> reverse Pereira and reverse Van Camp.

Reverse Pereira
- Time & skill of managing spouse greater factor in appreciation
- CP gets a fair rate of return on investment times years plus original investment; managing spouse gets remainder
- *Example*
  - Value of CP business at separation = $10,000
  - Number of years between separation & dissolution = 2
  - Value at dissolution = $100,000
  - CP gets 10% times $10,000 times 2 plus original investment (10,000) = $12,000
  - SP gets $100,000 - $12,000 = $88,000

Reverse Van Camp
- Economic conditions the greater factor in appreciation
- SP gets salary for reasonable value of services times years; CP gets the rest
- *Example*
  - Value of CP business at separation = $10,000
  - Number of years between separation & dissolution = 2
  - Value at dissolution = $100,000
  - Reasonable salary = $25,000 per year
  - SP gets $25,000 times 2 = $50,000 ——————— CP gets $100,000 - $50,000 or $50,000

[THIS PAGE INTENTIONALLY LEFT BLANK.]

IV. INVOLVEMENT OF THIRD PARTIES – debt arises when **contract is made**, at time tort occurs, or at the time other obligation arises

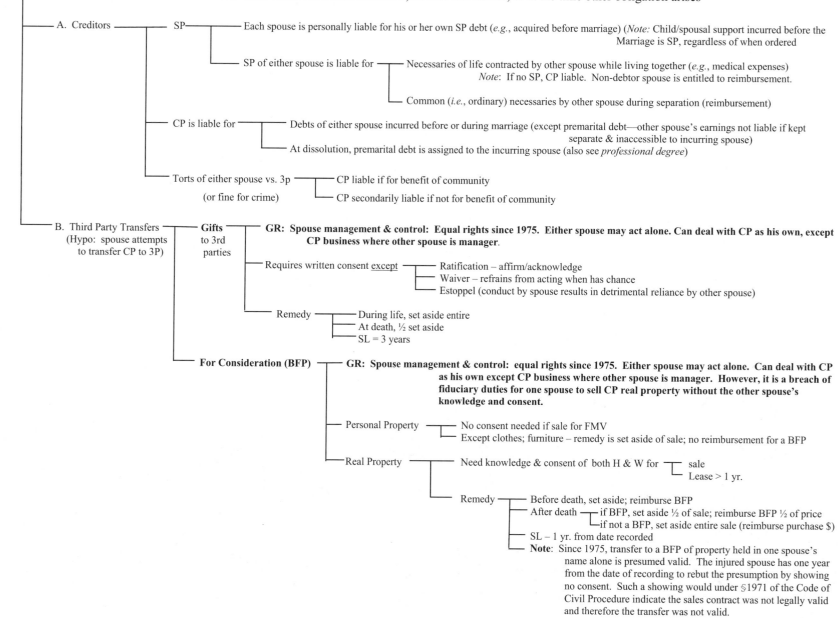

A. Creditors

- **SP**
  - Each spouse is personally liable for his or her own SP debt (*e.g.*, acquired before marriage) (*Note:* Child/spousal support incurred before the Marriage is SP, regardless of when ordered
  - SP of either spouse is liable for
    - Necessaries of life contracted by other spouse while living together (*e.g.*, medical expenses) *Note*: If no SP, CP liable. Non-debtor spouse is entitled to reimbursement.
    - Common (*i.e.*, ordinary) necessaries by other spouse during separation (reimbursement)
- **CP is liable for**
  - Debts of either spouse incurred before or during marriage (except premarital debt—other spouse's earnings not liable if kept separate & inaccessible to incurring spouse)
  - At dissolution, premarital debt is assigned to the incurring spouse (also see *professional degree*)
- **Torts of either spouse vs. 3p** (or fine for crime)
  - CP liable if for benefit of community
  - CP secondarily liable if not for benefit of community

B. Third Party Transfers (Hypo: spouse attempts to transfer CP to 3P)

- **Gifts to 3rd parties**
  - **GR: Spouse management & control: Equal rights since 1975. Either spouse may act alone. Can deal with CP as his own, except CP business where other spouse is manager.**
  - Requires written consent <u>except</u>
    - Ratification – affirm/acknowledge
    - Waiver – refrains from acting when has chance
    - Estoppel (conduct by spouse results in detrimental reliance by other spouse)
  - Remedy
    - During life, set aside entire
    - At death, ½ set aside
    - SL = 3 years
- **For Consideration (BFP)**
  - **GR: Spouse management & control: equal rights since 1975. Either spouse may act alone. Can deal with CP as his own except CP business where other spouse is manager. However, it is a breach of fiduciary duties for one spouse to sell CP real property without the other spouse's knowledge and consent.**
  - Personal Property
    - No consent needed if sale for FMV
    - Except clothes; furniture – remedy is set aside of sale; no reimbursement for a BFP
  - Real Property
    - Need knowledge & consent of both H & W for
      - sale
      - Lease > 1 yr.
    - Remedy
      - Before death, set aside; reimburse BFP
      - After death
        - if BFP, set aside ½ of sale; reimburse BFP ½ of price
        - if not a BFP, set aside entire sale (reimburse purchase $)
      - SL – 1 yr. from date recorded
      - **Note**: Since 1975, transfer to a BFP of property held in one spouse's name alone is presumed valid. The injured spouse has one year from the date of recording to rebut the presumption by showing no consent. Such a showing would under §1971 of the Code of Civil Procedure indicate the sales contract was not legally valid and therefore the transfer was not valid.

[THIS PAGE INTENTIONALLY LEFT BLANK.]

Example, Real Property Transfer without knowledge and consent:

Wife uses $50,000 of CP funds to buy a condominium in her name alone, without her husband's knowledge (and so, without his consent). Five years later, she sells the condominium for $100,000. The value of the property sky-rockets to $300,000 within a few weeks.

Hypothetical #1: Husband discovers the sale 6 months later (wife is still alive).

> Remedy: Husband can ask the court to set aside the sale of the condominium, reimburse the purchaser his $100,000 purchase price, and take title to the $300,000 condo. Note that the purchaser recovers his purchase price, but loses the entire appreciation.

Hypothetical #2: Wife dies and then Husband discovers existence and sale of the condominium, all within one year of the sale. The sale was to a BFP (*i.e.*, a purchaser who paid FMV and was unaware that Wife was married).

> Remedy: Husband can ask the court to set aside ½ of the sale (*i.e.*, his community property ½ of the condominium). Husband reimburses the BFP $50,000 (1/2 of his purchase price) and becomes a tenant in common with the BFP in the property. Husband then has title to ½ of the $300,000 condo. Note that the BFP then gets to keep ½ of the appreciation; husband gets the ½ that would have been his CP ½.

Hypothetical #3: Wife dies and then Husband discovers existence and sale of the condominium, all within one year of the sale. The sale was <u>not</u> to a BFP (*i.e.*, the purchaser paid less than FMV or was aware that Wife was married).

> Remedy: Husband can ask the court to set aside the entire sale of the condominium, reimburse the purchase price, and take title to the $300,000 condo.

V. DISTRIBUTION

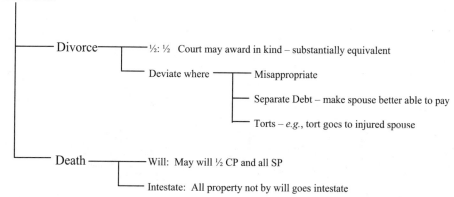

- Divorce
  - ½: ½   Court may award in kind – substantially equivalent
  - Deviate where
    - Misappropriate
    - Separate Debt – make spouse better able to pay
    - Torts – *e.g.*, tort goes to injured spouse
- Death
  - Will: May will ½ CP and all SP
  - Intestate: All property not by will goes intestate

[THIS PAGE INTENTIONALLY LEFT BLANK.]

Feb 2004
Question 2

In 1989, Herb and Wendy married while domiciled in Montana, a non-community property state. Prior to the marriage, Wendy had borrowed $25,000 from a Montana bank and had executed a promissory note in that amount in favor of the bank. Herb and Wendy, using savings from their salaries during their marriage, bought a residence, and took title to the residence as tenants in common.

In 1998, Herb and Wendy moved to California and became domiciled here. They did not sell their Montana house.

In 1999, Herb began having an affair with Ann. Herb told Ann that he intended to divorce Wendy and marry her (Ann), and suggested that they live together until dissolution proceedings were concluded. Ann agreed, and Herb moved in with her. Herb told Wendy that he was going to move into his own apartment because he "needed some space." Ann assumed Herb's last name, and Herb introduced her to his friends as his wife. Herb and Ann bought an automobile with a loan. They listed themselves as husband and wife on the loan application, and took title as husband and wife. Herb paid off the automobile loan out of his earnings.

In the meantime, Herb continued to spend occasional weekends with Wendy, who was unaware of Herb's relationship with Ann. Wendy urged Herb to consult a marriage counselor with her, which he did, but Herb did not disclose his relationship with Ann.

In 2003, Wendy and Ann learned the facts set forth in the preceding paragraphs. Wendy promptly filed a petition for dissolution of marriage, asserting a 50% interest in the Montana house and in the automobile. At the time of filing, the Montana bank was demanding payment of $8,000 as the past-due balance on Wendy's promissory note which has been reduced to a judgment. Also at the time of filing, Ann had a $15,000 bank account in her name alone, comprised solely of her earnings while she was living with Herb.

1. What rights do Herb, Wendy, and Ann each have in:
    a. The residence in Montana? Discuss.

    b. The automobile? Discuss.

    c. The $15,000 bank account? Discuss.

2. What property may the Montana bank reach to satisfy the past-due balance on Wendy's promissory note? Discuss.

Answer according to California law.

Model Answer
Dennis P. Saccuzzo & Nancy E. Johnson

1. (a) H's, W's & A's Rights in the Residence in Montana

California is a <u>community property</u> state. By California law, all property and debts acquired during a valid marriage are presumed to be community property (CP).

CA community property laws apply to married couples who move to California from another state. <u>Quasi-community property</u> (QCP) is property (wherever situated), acquired by a married couple in another jurisdiction that would have been CP if the acquiring spouse were domiciled in CA. QCP remains the separate property (SP) of the acquiring spouse except at the death of the acquiring spouse, dissolution of the marriage, or action by creditors.

All property and debts acquired before marriage, after permanent separation, by gift, or by inheritance, and all rents, income and profits therefrom, are considered the <u>separate property</u> (SP) of the acquiring spouse.

Putative Marriage Doctrine

California CP laws also apply to quasi-marital property (QMP), which is property acquired during a void or voidable marriage, which would have been CP or QCP if the marriage were not void or voidable.

California CP law does not recognize relationships where both spouses are aware that they are not in a marital relationship. It does recognize <u>putative marriages</u>, in which one of the spouses has a good faith belief in the existence of the marriage.

Herb told Ann that he intended to divorce W and marry her, so Ann knew about the existence of H's & W's marriage. Moreover, H suggested to Ann that Ann and H live together "until dissolution proceedings were concluded," and Ann agreed. Therefore, Ann maintained an awareness of the existence of the marriage while she and H were living together. It is irrelevant that Ann assumed H's last name, introduced Ann to his friends as his wife, and listed themselves as husband and wife on an auto loan because none of these acts show that Ann had a good faith belief in the existence of the marriage.

Herb was also well aware of his marriage. He lied to his wife about his affair and about moving in with Ann. He even went to a marriage counselor while he was living with Ann, and failed to disclose his relationship with Ann.

Because neither Ann nor H had a good faith belief in the existence of a marriage between them, there was no putative marriage. Neither will have a community property interest in the assets of the other, regardless of when acquired.

QCP

The Montana residence was purchased with savings from H & W's salaries during their marriage. Had H & W been domiciled in California, the savings would have been the fruits of H and W during marriage. Therefore, the savings are QCP because they would have been CP had H & W been domiciled in California.

Change in Form Doctrine

Change in form does not change the character of the property. The residence was purchased with a QCP asset. Therefore, the residence is also QCP.

Effect of Joint Title

Title is not controlling; interest is the key. H & W took title as tenants in common (TC), meaning that each owned an undivided equal share in the residence. Thus, the TC remained QCP.

At dissolution, QCP is treated as CP. Moreover, property held in joint form is treated as CP. Therefore, at dissolution the residence will be considered the CP of H & W and will be divided 50/50 between them. Ann receives nothing of the residence.

(b) The Automobile

Separation

Herb and Ann purchased the automobile with a loan while living together. They took title as husband and wife. H paid off the loan using his earnings. The first issue is whether H was separated from W during these transactions, because if he had been separated, his earnings and the car would be his separate property.

A permanent separation requires three elements: no intent to reconcile, physical separation, and communication to spouse of intent.

During the separation, H saw a marriage counselor, which would defeat his claim of no intent to reconcile. Moreover, H continued to spend occasional weekends with W, so his physical separation was partial at best. Finally, H never communicated his intent to separate to W. He told her he needed some space, and even failed to disclose his relationship with A during marriage counseling. Therefore, H did not perfect a separation.

Because H did not physically separate, the earnings he used to pay off the auto loan were CP.

Gifts to Third Parties

In California, the spouses have equal rights of management and control. Either can act alone, and can deal with CP as his/her own except for a CP business where the other spouse is the manager.

Nevertheless, a gift to a third party of CP funds requires written consent absent ratification, waiver, or estoppel. No facts indicate W found out about the auto before W paid for it, so none of the exceptions apply. Moreover, H certainly did not obtain written consent as he never told W about his relationship with Ann.

Given that H paid for the entire loan with CP funds without W's consent, any interest of Ann's in the auto must be construed as a gift of H & W's CP to Ann.

When a defrauded spouse learns of a gift of CP to a third party within the 3-year statute of limitations and while her spouse is alive, she can set aside the entire gift. Under the present facts, W can set aside the entire gift. Therefore, any interest Ann might claim would be set aside. H & Ann's taking title as husband and wife was fraudulent and will have no legal effect. Therefore, the auto will be CP and divided 50/50 between H and W. Ann has no interest.

(c) The Bank Account

The bank account was in Ann's name alone. The account was funded solely by her earnings while she was living with H.

Because there was no putative marriage (see above), the earnings and the account are Ann's SP. Neither H nor W have any interest in A's SP bank account.

In Sum

The residence is CP and will be divided 50/50 between H and W; Ann has no interest.

The auto is CP and will be divided 50/50 between H and W; Ann has no interest.

The bank account is Ann's SP; H and W have no interest.

2. W's Past Due Balance

W borrowed $25,000 from a Montana bank prior to marriage, so the source of the loan is SP. However, the bank received a judgment of $8,000 while H and W were still married.

SP Debt

Generally, each spouse is liable for his or her own SP debt. Therefore, W would have been liable for her own SP debt at dissolution. However, CP is generally liable for debts of either spouse incurred before or during the marriage. Because the judgment for $8,000 occurred during the marriage, the judgment can be construed as a CP debt, and therefore will not be assigned to W as an SP debt.

Conclusion: The Montana bank may reach the CP of H and W. The residence and auto are both CP of H and W, so the bank can put a lien on either. The bank cannot reach Ann's bank account because, as discussed, the account is Ann's SP.

February 2003
Question 6

Henry and Wanda married in 1980 when both were students at State X University. State X is a non-community property state. Shortly after the marriage, Henry graduated and obtained employment with a State X engineering firm. Wanda gave birth to the couple's only child, and Henry and Wanda agreed that Wanda would quit her job and remain home to care for the child. They bought a house in State X using their savings for the down payment and obtained a loan secured by a twenty-year mortgage for the balance of the purchase price. Mortgage payments were subsequently paid from Henry's earnings. The title to the State X house was in Henry's name alone.

In 1990, Henry accepted a job offer from a California engineering firm. The couple moved to California with their child and rented out the State X house.

In 1992, Wanda's uncle died and left her an oil painting with an appraised value of $5,000 and a small cabin located on a lake in California. Wanda took the painting to the cabin and hung it over the fireplace.

In 1993, after reading a book entitled "How to Avoid Probate," Henry persuaded Wanda to execute and record a deed conveying the lake cabin to "Henry and Wanda, as joint tenants with right of survivorship." Wanda did so, believing that the only effect of the conveyance would be to avoid probate.

In 1995, after three years of study paid for out of Henry's earnings, Wanda obtained a degree in podiatry and opened her own podiatry practice. Her practice became quite successful because of her enthusiasm, skill, and willingness to work long hours. Henry continued to work for the engineering firm.

In 2002, Henry and Wanda separated and filed for dissolution of marriage. Wanda had the painting reappraised. The artist, now deceased, has become immensely popular, and the painting is now worth $50,000.

Upon dissolution, what are Henry's and Wanda's respective rights in:

1. The lake cabin? Discuss.

2. The painting? Discuss.

3. The State X house? Discuss.

4. Wanda's professional education and podiatry practice? Discuss.

Answer according to California law.

-- Written by Dennis P. Saccuzzo & Nancy E. Johnson

Commentary:

The key to writing a better community property answer is to raise as many issues as possible, given the facts. Generally the answer should begin with basic definitions such as community property (CP), separate property (SP) and quasi-community property (QCP) where the fact pattern stipulates a marriage in a non-community property state. It is essential that definitions are thorough and precise.

Once the definitional issues are dispensed with, the best answers begin by identifying the original source of the property as being SP, CP, or QCP. The next step is to carefully trace each and every event and related issue relevant to a possible change in character of the property. To illustrate these principles, we will discuss each of the 4 calls of this question.

(1) The lake cabin. The source of the lake cabin is SP because Wanda inherited it from her uncle in 1992. At that time W and H were married and living in California, so California community property laws apply. The next relevant event was that Henry persuaded Wanda to execute and record a deed changing title to the property to a joint tenancy. The first rule invoked by this change is the general rule that change in form does not affect the character of the property. Another rule is that title is not controlling: interest is the key. The basic issue we must confront is whether the change in title effectuated a change in the character of the property.

Whenever one of the spouses takes action that might result in a change of character, the first thing that must be argued is gift and transmutation. Naturally, H will argue that when W changed title and conveyed the cabin to H and W as joint tenants, W's act was either a gift or transmutation of the property from W's separate property to a joint tenancy. The rule is that gifts/transmutations require a writing by express declaration. H's argument is that the conveyance satisfies the writing requirement, and this is an important issue because he does have a colorable claim.

Given H's possible claim of a valid gift or transmutation, the next rule invoked is that property taken in joint form is presumed to be CP at dissolution. A reading of the facts indicates that treating the cabin as CP would not be fair because it was H who convinced W to execute the conveyance and W believed the only effect would be to avoid probate. The problem then is what can we reasonably do for W?

If the transmutation theory is valid, then what occurred was a transmutation of SP to CP. The rule is that SP can be converted to CP without consideration. Whenever SP funds are converted to CP, it raises the rules in Lucas/anti-Lucas, as indicated in both of the selected answers provided by the Bar. Under the old rule in Lucas, the transfer would be construed as a gift. However, under anti-Lucas legislation, the SP funds would be entitled to reimbursement. Applying the anti-Lucas legislation, W would be entitled to reimbursement of her original SP contribution to the cabin. The community would split whatever appreciation had accrued.

The problem with giving H even half of the appreciation, if any, is that it was he who persuaded W to execute the deed and there is at least a hint that he acted in bad faith. Better answers would have discussed this possible bad faith as well as W's belief and intent that the conveyance would merely avoid probate, and argue that H should receive nothing.

2. _The painting_. The source of the painting is SP because W inherited it from her uncle in 1992, while the couple were married and living in California. W took the painting to the cabin and hung it over the fireplace. Because W believed she owned the cabin, there is no indication that she attempted to transmute the painting to CP, and there is no writing by express declaration. In 2002, 10 years later, the painting had appreciated from $5000 to $50,000 because the artist had died and become immensely popular. These facts indicate that the appreciation was due to economic factors rather than to any skill or labor by W. The property therefore remains W's separate property.

Although neither of the Bar's selected answers raised Pereira/Van Camp, it was possible to do so under these facts because the painting was a SP asset that, construed broadly, could be considered a business that appreciated during the marriage. There was an opportunity to show one's knowledge and understanding of California community laws by discussing the rules in both Pereira and Van Camp and concluding that at best the rule in Van Camp would apply because the appreciation was due to economic factors. Under Van Camp, the community is entitled to only a reasonable salary for the efforts of the owner spouse, and because W did nothing but hang the painting over fireplace, the community gets nothing. The painting is Wanda's. Good answers to this question would have discussed Pereira/Van Camp either here or in call 4.

3. _The State X house_. The State X house was purchased in a non-CP state, so QCP rules are implicated. Whenever QCP is implicated, the first question we must ask is whether the asset or debt would have been CP had the parties been domiciled in California. Here the facts indicate that their savings were used for a down payment. Because the couple's savings would have been CP had the couple been domiciled in California, the down payment is QCP. The couple obtained a mortgage loan, which raises the rule of intent of the lender. Because this was a house for a husband and wife, the intent of the lender would no doubt be to look to both parties for repayment and therefore the loan would have been a community debt had the parties been domiciled in California.

Mortgage payments were made from H's earnings. Earnings during the marriage are considered CP, therefore, had the couple been domiciled in California the earnings would have been CP. In sum, the down payment and funds to pay the mortgage are QCP because they would have been CP had the parties been domiciled in California. The fact that title was taken in H's name alone raises the rule that title is not controlling: interest is the key. Here the house was purchased with funds that would have been CP had the couple been domiciled in California, so the house would be a QCP asset even though its title was in H's name alone.

As a community asset, the property would be divided 50/50. One of the Bar's selected answers raised the issue of jurisdiction of the California court over out-of-state property. This is the first time this issue has appeared in the California Bar's selected answers to CP questions. Because this discussion appeared in only one of the two selected answers, its inclusion was obviously not necessary for a high *score. Nevertheless, as the Bar's selected answer indicates, the solution is simple. The court can divide property in kind and give W the value for the State X house from funds held in California or even exercise its personal jurisdiction over H and if necessary create a constructive trust. Please note that the rules for out-of-state property are different in a dissolution as opposed to a death. Under the California Probate Code, the California court would not have jurisdiction over the out-of-state real property, and this issue has not been tested on the California Bar as of July 2003.*

4. <u>Wanda's professional education and podiatry practice.</u> Notice that call 4 really involves 2 separate questions. This is a common practice on the California Bar exam, and a common mistake is to respond to only one of the two. The rules pertaining to professional education have been tested repeatedly on the California Bar exam. It is necessary to point out in your answer that the professional degree remains the SP of the acquiring spouse. The next issue that must be discussed is reimbursement and the 10-year rule. California law provides for reimbursement where the professional degree substantially enhances the earning capacity of the acquiring spouse. Here, that is not an issue because a podiatry practice would no doubt accomplish that.

Generally the community is entitled to reimbursement only for educational expenses but not for living expenses. The next issue that must be discussed is the 10-year rule, which presumes that if the degree has been held for more than 10 years, the community has gotten the benefit of the education and is not entitled to reimbursement. Past Bar questions have varied the number of years in which the acquiring spouse held the degree during the existence of the community. Here, W had the degree from 1995 until 2002, or about 7 years, therefore the presumption would not apply. Interestingly, one of the Bar's selected answers argued that the community had benefited for 7 years and so should be entitled to reimbursement for 3/10 of the educational expenses. Notice that the education expenses were paid for out of H's earnings, which would make the payments CP.

The podiatry practice was started during the existence of the community and so is a community asset. Therefore the value of the business, including any goodwill, should be split 50/50 at dissolution. However, the fact pattern presents facts that would usually lead one to analyze Pereira/Van Camp: that the practice became successful because of W's enthusiasm, skill, and willingness to work long hours. Had the practice been a separate property business, then Pereira/Van Camp would have been triggered and the rule in Pereira would have been triggered under these facts. It is particularly important for Bar candidates to note that both of the Bar's selected answers provided a detailed discussion of Pereira/Van Camp, even though this was not a Pereira/Van Camp situation. The best explanation for the apparent credit received is that, as with our discussion of the painting (above), there were facts relevant to Pereira/Van Camp and that is what justified the discussion. As indicated, some discussion of Pereira/Van Camp either here or in call 2 appeared to be mandatory.

An important final point is that facts triggered reverse Pereira/Van Camp. Reverse Pereira/Van Camp is triggered in the situation in which there is a CP business that appreciates after permanent separation and before final dissolution. The call of the question asked about rights of the parties at dissolution. They separated in 2002, but if W continues her practice, and her enthusiasm, skill, and long hours cause further appreciation before final dissolution, then reverse Pereira would apply, as discussed in the following model.

California is a community property state. All property and debts acquired during the existence of the marriage are presumed to be community property. Henry and Wanda were married in 1980, moved to California in 1990, and filed for dissolution of the marriage in 2002 while domiciled in California. The division of their property will be governed by California community property (CP) laws.

According to California CP laws, separate property is all property and debts acquired before marriage, after permanent separation, by gift, or by inheritance plus all rents, income and profits that derive from these sources. Facts indicate that Wanda inherited property during the marriage, so separate property rules will apply.

Quasi community property (QCP) is all property (wherever situated) and debts acquired by a married couple in another jurisdiction that would have been CP if the acquiring spouse had been domiciled in California. Henry and Wanda were married in 1980 in State X, a non-community property state, before moving to California in 1990. Therefore, the rules pertaining to QCP will apply. QCP is not the same thing as CP. It remains the SP of the acquiring spouse except at the acquiring spouse's death, at dissolution, and in action by creditors. At dissolution it will be divided like CP. Because the issue is what are Henry and Wanda's respective rights in various assets acquired during their marriage, at dissolution any QCP will be divided as though it were CP.

The Lake Cabin

The original source of the lake cabin is SP because Wanda inherited from her uncle in 1992 and, as indicated, property acquired by inheritance is SP.

Transmutation/Gift

Property rights may be altered (transmuted) by agreement without consideration. When Wanda executed and recorded a deed conveying the lake cabin to "Henry and Wanda as joint tenants with right of survivorship," she effected a transmutation of her separate property to a joint tenancy. In a joint tenancy each tenant owns a distinct equal undivided interest in the property. Each has the right to sell or devise his or her share. At the death of one of the joint tenants, the effect of right of survivorship is that the surviving spouse takes the entire estate by operation of law.

<u>Requirement of a Writing</u>: Since 1985, California law has required that <u>transmutations</u> must be in writing by express declaration. The writing must expressly state that the characterization of property is being changed. The requirement for a writing also applies to gifts as of July 1987 unless the gift is of a personal nature and not substantial in value given the marriage. The lake cabin is not personal and probably is of substantial value so a writing would be required whether the conveyance is characterized as a transmutation or gift. Therefore, the requisite writing will be required.

Facts indicate that Wanda executed and recorded a deed conveying the lake cabin. Because it is an interest in real property, the deed is covered by the Statute of Frauds and requires a writing. The writing must indicate the identity of the parties, give a description of the property, and be signed by the party to be charged.

Assuming that the deed was valid, it should satisfy the writing requirement for transmutation and gifts because it clearly changed the character of the property from Wanda's SP to a joint tenancy. Therefore the conveyance is a valid gift or transmutation.

Wanda's erroneous belief that the only effect of the conveyance was to avoid probate and the fact that Henry persuaded Wanda to execute and record the deed will probably not help Wanda because no facts indicate fraud or scienter on Henry's part, and although Wanda did not seem to have the intent to transmute, the written and recorded deed will probably prevail.

Further, under California CP laws, property taken in joint form is presumed to be CP at dissolution. Because Wanda now faces dissolution, she has effectively transmuted the lake cabin from her SP to CP. The next issue is whether Wanda has any recourse under California CP laws.

Lucas/Anti-Lucas

Under the old rule in Lucas, when SP funds are used toward the purchase or acquisition of joint property, the SP funds were presumed to be a gift to the community absent an agreement to the contrary. However, under the modern anti-Lucas legislation, such SP funds are entitled to reimbursement of the principal dollar for dollar, absent an agreement to the contrary. No facts indicate an agreement for Wanda not to be reimbursed, so she will be entitled to reimbursement of the fair market value of the lake cabin at the time of the conveyance. The community will then split only any appreciation. If the appreciation is significant, Wanda can argue that she lacked intent to transmute the property or that it was done at Henry's urging, and possibly examine a possible fraud or misrepresentation theory. As indicated, however, these theories probably will not be successful.

The Painting

Wanda also inherited the painting, so its original source is SP. She hung the painting over the fireplace in her SP cabin, which she believed was hers even after the conveyance, so there is no indication of a gift or transmutation. Moreover, there is no writing by express declaration to suggest a gift theory. Any argument by Henry that the painting was a <u>fixture</u> that was transmuted along with the lake cabin would fail: paintings are not so affixed to the property as to become part of the land. The original value of the painting was $5,000, but at separation the painting had appreciated to $50,000.

<u>Pereira/Van Camp</u>

When a separate property business appreciates during the existence of a community, the California courts will apply the rules in Pereira or Van Camp to determine whether the community is entitled to a share of the appreciation. Broadly speaking, any SP asset that appreciates during the existence of the community can be construed as a separate property business, and Henry can request the court to apply these doctrines to receive a share of the $45,000 appreciation.

Under the rule in <u>Pereira</u>, where the time and skill of the owner spouse is the greater factor in the appreciation, the SP gets a fair rate of return on the original investment times the number of years married plus the original investment, and the community gets everything else.

Under the rule in <u>Van Camp</u>, if business or economic factors produce the profits, the community gets a salary for a reasonable value of the services of the owner spouse, and the SP gets everything else.

Facts are clear in indicating that the appreciation was in no way due to Wanda's time and skill. All she did was hang the painting in her cabin after she inherited it. The appreciation was due solely to the fact that the artist, now deceased, had become immensely popular. Therefore, assuming the painting is treated as a SP business, the court would apply the formula in Van Camp and the CP would be entitled to only a reasonable value of Wanda's services. Because all she did was hang the painting, the community would be entitled to little or nothing. Therefore the painting is all Wanda's.

The State X House

The State X house was acquired while Henry and Wanda were domiciled in State X and before they moved to California. It was acquired by using Henry and Wanda's savings as a down payment. Because the couple's savings would have been CP had they been domiciled in California, the down payment is QCP. The couple took out a mortgage loan for the balance. Because this was a house for husband and wife, the <u>intent of the lender</u> would no doubt be to look to both parties for repayment, so the loan would have been a CP debt had they been domiciled in California. Finally, mortgage payments were made from Henry's earnings. Earnings during the marriage are considered CP in California, therefore the funds to pay off the debt were also QCP.

In sum, the down payment and funds to pay the mortgage on the State X house are QCP. Therefore, the source of the house is QCP.

<u>Effect of Title in Henry's Name</u>

That title was taken in Henry's name alone is not dispositive. Title is not controlling; interest is the key. Here the house was purchased with QCP funds, so the house remains QCP.

<u>Transmutation/Gift</u>

Henry will argue that because Wanda allowed Henry to put title in his name alone, this was a gift or transmutation. However, unlike the conveyance of the lake cabin, there is no writing by express declaration changing the character of the property. Therefore, an argument based on gift or transmutation will fail and the State X house remains QCP.

<u>Distribution of State X House</u>

At dissolution, QCP is treated as CP and generally will be divided equally. As QCP, the State X house should be equally divided. The fact that the house is outside of California is not a problem because the California Family Code gives the courts power over out-of-state real property that is QCP. The court may distribute in kind, giving Wanda the value of her share of the house in other CP assets, or it can use its jurisdiction over Henry and create a constructive trust so that Wanda will get her share.

Wanda's Professional Education and Podiatry Practice

Professional Education

Under California CP laws, a professional degree or license remains the SP of the acquiring spouse. Therefore, Wanda's education and degree remain her SP; Henry has no share. However, if the education or training substantially enhances the earning capacity of the educated spouse, the community may be entitled to reimbursement for tuition and books. However, the community would generally not be entitled to reimbursement for living expenses.

Facts indicate that Wanda had a successful practice after having been a stay-at-home wife and mother, leaving little doubt that her education substantially enhanced her earning capacity. Therefore, the community may be entitled to reimbursement for CP contribution to Wanda's education and books. The educational expenses were paid for by Henry's earnings during the marriage. Hence, CP funds were in fact used.

However, there is a time limit on reimbursement. After 10 years, the community is presumed to have received the benefit of the education and would not be entitled to reimbursement. Here, Wanda obtained her degree in 1995 and maintained her practice through the dissolution in 2002, for a total of 7 years. Because her practice was successful, she has a good argument that the community has already received the benefit of her education, or at least should receive no more than a pro rata share of reimbursement based on 10 years (3/10 of the educational costs). This would be a matter of court discretion.

The Podiatry Practice

The practice was initiated during the existence of the community and is therefore a community asset. As such, the fair market value, including goodwill, will be divided 50/50 at dissolution. The <u>Pereira/Van Camp rules</u> discussed above would not apply. These doctrines apply to a SP asset that appreciates. Here there is a CP asset that will be split 50/50.

<u>Reverse Pereira/Van Camp</u>

The issue is what are Henry's and Wanda's respective rights in the practice at dissolution. Henry and Wanda separated in 2002, but the dissolution won't take place for at least 6 more months, and possibly much longer if there is a battle over the assets and child custody. No doubt Wanda will continue her practice through final dissolution.

After permanent separation but before dissolution, if a CP business managed by one of the spouses after separation continues to appreciate, the courts will apply the rules in reverse Pereira/Van Camp.

Reverse Pereira will be applied where the time and skill of the managing spouse is the greater factor in the appreciation. In this circumstance, the community gets a fair rate of return on the investment plus the original investment and the managing spouse gets the remainder.

Reverse Van Camp will be applied when economic conditions are the greater factor in the appreciation. Then the managing spouse gets a salary for the reasonable value of her services and CP gets the rest.

Facts indicate that Wanda's practice became successful because of her enthusiasm, skill and willingness to work long hours. If such efforts cause the value of the practice to continue to appreciate between the separation in 2002 and the final dissolution, the court will apply the rule in reverse Pereira. The fair market value of the practice at dissolution will be determined, and the community will receive a fair rate of return on the investment plus the original investment at dissolution. If, on the other hand, Wanda is unable to put in as much effort because of the divorce or responsibilities as a single parent and the value of the practice increases due to economic factors, then Wanda will receive a reasonable salary for the value of her services during the separation period, and the community will get the remainder.

[THIS PAGE INTENTIONALLY LEFT BLANK.]

In 1997, Hank and Wanda, both domiciled in Illinois, a non-community property state, began dating regularly. Hank, an attorney, told Wanda that Illinois permits common-law marriage. Hank knew this statement was false, but Wanda reasonably believed him. In 1998, Wanda moved in with Hank and thought she was validly married to him. They used Hank's earnings to cover living expenses. Wanda deposited all her earnings in a savings account she opened and maintained in her name alone.

In February 2000, Hank and Wanda moved to California and became domiciled here. By that time Wanda's account contained $40,000. She used the $40,000 to buy a parcel of land in Illinois and took title in her name alone.

Shortly after their arrival in California, Wanda inherited an expensive sculpture. Hank bought a marble pedestal for their apartment and told Wanda it was "so we can display our sculpture." They both frequently referred to the sculpture as "our collector's prize."

In March 2000, a woman who claimed Hank was the father of her 6 year-old child filed a paternity suit against Hank in California. In September 2000, the court determined Hank was the child's father and ordered him to pay $800 per month as child support.

In January 2002, Wanda discovered that she never has been validly married to Hank. Hank moved out of the apartment he shared with Wanda.

Hank has not paid the attorney who defended him in the paternity case. Hank paid the ordered child support for three months from his earnings but has paid nothing since.

1. What are Hank's and Wanda's respective rights in the parcel of land and the sculpture? Discuss.

2. Which of the property set forth in the facts can be reached to satisfy the obligations to pay child support and the attorney's fees? Discuss.

Answer according to California law.

JULY 2002, QUESTION 6

-- Written by Dennis P. Saccuzzo & Nancy E. Johnson

Commentary:

The calls of the question structure this answer. Call 1 asks for H's and W's rights in 2 specific assets, the parcel of land and the sculpture. As always, when the Bar gives you more than one asset or item to discuss, there will be some important distinction between or among them. For example, as seen below, the parcel could be construed as CP but the sculpture was SP.

Call 2 asks for a discussion of creditor rights, again specifically for 2 types of creditors: child support and professional services (attorney fees). Again, there were important distinctions that lead to different conclusions for each of the 2 types of creditors.

Frequently, in order to be responsive to a question, a number of issues not specifically called for must be addressed. In community property, one must always address CP versus SP, and often there is an issue of quasi-community property (QCP). This question presented the additional wrinkle of quasi-marital property (QMP) that also required a discussion of putative marriage in the unsettled area of the law regarding a fraudulent spouse in a putative marriage.

A very common mistake made by many students is to over-simplify community property questions and thereby miss subtle issues. The general approach to CP questions is to consider the original source of each asset or debt (e.g., SP or CP. For QCP, it is necessary to determine whether any asset or debt would have been CP or SP had the parties been domiciled in California and to always remember that QCP remains the SP of the acquiring spouse until death of the acquiring spouse, dissolution, or action by creditors.

Once the source has been determined, then it is important to look at any presumptions that affect the character of the property (e.g., title is not conclusive – interest is the key) as well as any action by the parties that may affect the character (e.g., gift or transmutation). It is important to carefully discuss each of the presumptions and actions in the fact pattern that might affect character, to show your thinking, as opposed to jumping to a conclusion without showing the steps that caused you to arrive at it.

As the following answer illustrates, it was important here to apply California community property laws even though there was a bad-faith partner for whom the court may not have applied CP laws. In CP questions the Bar is always testing your knowledge of California CP laws, regardless of how the question is framed.

Call 1: H's & W's rights in parcel and sculpture

California is a <u>community property</u> state. By California law, all property and debts acquired during a valid marriage are presumed to be community property (CP).

CA community property laws apply to married couples who move to California from another state. <u>Quasi-community property</u> (QCP) is property (wherever situated), acquired by a married couple in another jurisdiction that would have been CP if the acquiring spouse were domiciled in CA. QCP remains the separate property (SP) of the acquiring spouse except at the death of the acquiring spouse, dissolution of the marriage, or action by creditors.

All property and debts acquired before marriage, after permanent separation, by gift, or by inheritance, and all rents, income and profits therefrom, are considered the <u>separate property</u> (SP) of the acquiring spouse.

Quasi-Marital Property (QMP)/Putative Marriage

California CP laws also apply to QMP, which is property acquired during a void or voidable marriage, which would have been CP or QCP if the marriage were not void or voidable.

California CP law does not recognize relationships where both spouses are aware that they are not in a marital relationship. It does recognize <u>putative marriages</u> where one of the spouses has a good faith belief in the existence of the marriage.

Hank (H), an attorney, told Wanda (W) that Illinois, the state in which they resided, permitted common law marriages. Even though Hank's statement was false, facts state that W reasonably believed him. Given that H was an attorney, W's belief does in fact appear to be reasonable. Therefore, W had a good faith belief in the existence of the marriage, and California CP laws will apply. W is an innocent or putative spouse. H's fraud and knowledge that no marriage existed would not negate the existence of a putative marriage, and the jurisdiction of the CA courts. Because H did not have a good faith belief in the existence of a marriage, he is a bad faith partner and not considered a putative spouse.

The general rule is that upon dissolution of a putative marriage, the courts shall treat QMP as CP or QCP, which means the property will be equally divided. The law is unsettled, however, as to whether the bad faith spouse has a right to invoke the putative marriage doctrine to demand equal division; the courts are divided on this issue. Here, the good faith spouse (W) has no reason to invoke the doctrine because all of the property in question is in her name or is her SP, as discussed below. When H attempts to invoke the doctrine to satisfy creditors, the court may decide to invoke and treat property as QCP/CP, or refuse to invoke and allow the property to remain W's SP.

If the court does not allow H to invoke putative marriage doctrine, then H will have no right to either the parcel or the sculpture; both will be W's SP. If, however, the court allows H to invoke the doctrine, the following analysis will apply.

The Parcel

W deposited her earnings in a savings account that she opened and maintained in her name alone. Had they been domiciled in California, this would have been considered CP. Under CA CP laws, title is not conclusive; interest is controlling. Because W's earnings were acquired during the existence of the putative marriage, they would have been considered CP. Although at the time they were domiciled in Illinois, a non-community property state, when H and W moved to CA in Feb 2000, the $40,000 would be treated as QMP.

Change in form does not change the character of the property. When W used the $40,000 in QMP to buy the parcel of land, the change in form did not affect the character of the parcel as QMP. Because interest rather than title is controlling, the fact that W took title in her name alone will not change the character of the parcel as QMP.

<u>Married Woman's Presumption and Transmutation</u>

The married woman's presumption, which presumes that title held as SP by a married woman <u>is</u> her SP, will not apply here because this presumption applies only to transactions prior to 1975. Here, W acquired the parcel in Feb 2000.

W's argument that the parcel was a gift or transmutation of the property from QMP to W's SP will also fail. Since 1985 transmutations of property, though legal without consideration, require a writing by express declaration indicating the change in form of the property. Since July 1987, gifts require an express declaration. Facts do not indicate any express declaration changing the character of the property, and the Feb 2000 acquisition of the parcel was well after the requirement of the writing.

Conclusion: Although H moved out, the facts are silent as to whether either party filed for dissolution and property division, or whether creditors forced such an action. Assuming a dissolution and application of putative marriage doctrine, Parcel is QMP and will be treated as CP on dissolution because it was acquired in CA during the existence of the putative marriage. H and W will each have a ½ interest, and the property may be subject to creditors' claims as discussed below. However, courts have the power to deviate from 50/50 distribution where there is fraud or misrepresentation, as is the case here.

Sculpture

W inherited the sculpture, therefore it is her separate property as defined above.

Transmutation

As indicated, in CA the spouses are free to transmute property from SP to CP. H's argument that W transmuted the property to CP will fail because of the absence of a writing by express declaration. Further, it was H who attempted to effectuate the transmutation by buying the marble pedestal and telling W it was "so we can display <u>our</u> [emphasis added] sculpture." If a transmutation was to be valid, it would have had to have been W, not H, who effectuated the transmutation. For similar reasons, a gift theory will fail as well.

Therefore, the sculpture will be treated as W's SP. It will be 100% W's except for possible creditor interests. H will have no rights to it, even under putative spouse doctrine.

Call 2: Obligations to Pay Child Support and Attorney Fees

Child Support

A child support debt arising outside the marriage, regardless of when ordered, is considered a debt incurred before marriage. At dissolution, any remaining child support debts will therefore be assigned to H. The issue is whether CP or W's SP will be liable for the one year of child support in arrears during the putative marriage, given that H paid the support for only 3 months.

CP Liability (the parcel)

Each spouse is personally liable for his or her own debt. However, CP is liable for the debts of either spouse incurred before or during the marriage until the time of dissolution.

It was determined that H had a six year old child in March of 2000. Because his putative marriage began in 1997, only 3 years prior to the determination, the duty to pay child support arose prior to the existence of the putative marriage and should be H's SP debt. If H has no SP, then CP would ordinarily be liable for the debt during the putative marriage. However, California CP laws will protect W.

A spouse's earnings (compensation for personal services) during marriage are not liable for the premarital debts of the other spouse if (1) the other spouse has no right to withdraw them and (2) the funds remain uncommingled. Facts indicate that W purchased parcel from her earnings deposited in a savings account opened and maintained in her name alone, indicating that H had no access to the funds. W used money from that account to purchase the parcel in her name alone, keeping it inaccessible to H. Further, facts indicate that H's earnings were used to cover living expenses, which would indicate he did not contribute funds toward the purchase of the parcel and there was no commingling. Therefore, because change in form does not change the character of the property, W's rights in the parcel should be exempted from liability for the unpaid child support. Only H's CP will therefore be liable. Moreover, the community is entitled to reimbursement from H's SP funds (if any) for the 3 months of child support paid during the putative marriage.

SP Liability (the sculpture)

Each spouse is personally liable for his or her own SP debt. Because the child support is H's SP debt, H's SP will be liable, as will the CP with the exception noted above.

Generally, a non-debtor spouse's SP cannot be reached to satisfy the debtor spouse's SP debt. However, the exception is that the SP of either spouse is liable for necessaries contracted by the other spouse while living together and common (ordinary) necessaries by the other spouse during separation. Necessaries refer to services and goods needed by the other spouse or his family for sustenance, such as food, shelter, medical care and dental care. The issue is whether the child support payments during the putative marriage were necessaries contracted during the marriage.

California has a strong public policy favoring child support, which can be argued to be a necessary because it provides sustenance to H's child. Although the child support judgment was made during the marriage and arguably is a necessary, as a matter of law such obligations are treated as a debt incurred before the marriage, regardless of when ordered. W's separate property should not be reachable to satisfy this debt.

Attorney Fees

As indicated, CP is liable for the debts of either spouse incurred during the marriage. H incurred the attorney fees during the marriage so H's attorney will have a claim against the parcel, which is CP, as discussed, if the court allows H to invoke the putative spouse doctrine.

Attorney will also argue that her fees were necessaries, and thereby attempt to make a claim on W's SP sculpture. Although arguable, it is unlikely that H's paternity suit will be considered a necessary of H.

Feb 2001

Question 1

In 1980, Herb married Wanda, and the couple took up residence in a California home, which Herb had purchased in 1979.

Herb had bought the home for $50,000 by making a $5,000 down payment and signing a promissory note for the balance. At the time of the marriage, the outstanding balance on this note was $44,000. During the next 20 years, the couple paid off the note by making payments from the combined salaries. The home now has a fair market value of $200,000.

In 1985, Wanda sold for $10,000 a watercolor she had painted that year. She and Herb orally agreed that the $10,000 would be her sole and separate property. Wanda invested the $10,000 in a mutual fund in her name alone. The current value of the mutual fund is $45,000.

In 1995, Herb and Wanda bought a vacation cabin on the California coast for $75,000. They made a down payment of $25,000 with community property funds, and both signed a note secured by a deed of trust on the cabin for the balance. Title to the cabin was taken in the names of both Herb and Wanda "as joint tenants."

Shortly afterward, Herb inherited a large sum of money from his mother and used $50,000 of his inheritance to pay off the note on the cabin. In 2000, Herb and Wanda added a room to the cabin at a cost of $20,000, which Herb paid out of the funds he had inherited. The current fair market value of the cabin is $150,000.

In 2001, Wanda instituted a dissolution proceeding. What are Herb's and Wanda's respective rights to:

1. The home? Discuss.
2. The mutual fund? Discuss.
3. The cabin? Discuss.

Answer according to California law.

COMMUNITY PROPERTY

February 2001 California Bar – Question 1

Answer Written by Professor Dennis P. Saccuzzo

CALL 1 – The Home

<u>Separate Property</u>

<u>Separate property</u> is all property and debts acquired before marriage, after permanent separation, by gift, or by inheritance and all income and profits that derive from these sources. California courts have explicitly held that property purchased by one spouse before marriage is separate property.

Herb and Wanda were married in 1980. Herb had purchased the residence in 1979. Because he acquired the home one year before marriage, the home is his separate property. It can be presumed that Herb took title to the home in his name alone because the facts state Herb had purchased the home.

Community Property Contribution to Home

Herb bought the home for $50,000. He made a $5,000 down payment and signed a promissory note. By the time of his marriage in 1980, he had paid another $1,000 toward the principal, and owed a balance of $44,000. During the next 20 years (1980-2000), the couple paid off the note from their combined salaries.

<u>Community Property</u>

All property and debts acquired during marriage are presumed <u>community property</u>. The couple's salaries were acquired during the marriage and therefore are community property. As such, community funds were used to pay the note.

<u>Moore Rule</u>

When a residence is purchased before marriage, title is taken in the purchasing spouse's name alone, and CP funds are used to pay down the mortgage as here, the rule in Moore applies. Under this rule the community is entitled to a pro rata share of the appreciation plus its contribution. The home remains Herb's separate property but the community has an interest in it by virtue of the community property payments made during the course of the parties' marriage.

Here, the current value of the home is $200,000. The original cost was $50,000. Hence, the house has appreciated $150,000 since Herb purchased it in 1979. The community contribution was 44,000/50,000 or 44/50. Thus, the community is entitled to 44/50 times $150,000 plus its $44,000 contribution, or $132,000 + $44,000 = $176,000. H and W will each get ½ of this amount.

Herb's separate property share will be 6/50 of the appreciation of $150,000, plus his $6,000 contribution. 6/50 times $150,000 = $18,000. $18,000 plus $6,000 gives a total of $24,000 in H's SP.

CALL 2. The Mutual Fund

Wanda painted a watercolor in 1985, which she sold for $10,000. Because the $10,000 was acquired during marriage as a result of Wanda's skill and labor, the proceeds are presumptively community property.

Transmutation

Under California community property law, the spouses can transmute property to each other without consideration (for example, community property can be transmuted to separate property). Prior to 1985, oral agreements proved by conduct generally prevailed; no formal requirements were enforced. From 1985 to the present, however, agreements must be in writing by express declaration, which means the writing must expressly state that the characterization of the property is being changed.

In 1985, H and W orally agreed that the $10,000 would be her sole separate property. Because this occurred in 1985, the oral agreement is insufficient. No facts indicate an express declaration. The attempted transmutation of community property to W's separate property fails, and the $10,000 would remain community property.

Gift

An exception to the requirement of an express written declaration is a gift prior to July 1987 or a gift after July 1987 that is either an item of a personal nature or not substantial in value given the marriage. Wanda will argue that the $10,000 was not a transmutation but rather a gift. For gifts, a writing was not required by the legislature until July 1987. Because the exchange was made in 1985, Wanda can attempt to get around the writing requirement. However, no facts indicate that this was a gift from Herb to Wanda and so the courts will probably call this a transmutation. Further, $10,000 is not personal in nature, and appears to be substantial in value relative to this marriage since it is about 1/5th of the original purchase price of the home. Thus, W has no way around the writing requirement, and the $10,000 is community property.

Tracing and the Exchange Rule

According to the exchange rule, change in form does not alter the character of the property. If the $10,000 was community property, then when Wanda used that money to purchase mutual funds the mutual funds were also community property.

Even assuming the court held that the $10,000 was W's separate property, H could make a claim on the appreciation that occurred on this asset by applying the formulas under Pereira/Van Camp.

Pereira/Van Camp

Facts indicate W invested the $10,000 in a mutual fund. The fund has appreciated, and its current value is now $45,000, for an appreciation of $35,000.

Pereira/Van Camp applies to a separate property business during the existence of the marriage. If the $10,000 was W's SP, then the mutual fund can be viewed as an SP business. Under the formula in Pereira, SP gets a fair rate of return on the original investment times the number of years the investment is held while married plus the original investment. The couple has held the investment for 15 years (1985 – 2000). Assuming 5% interest, 5% of $10,000 times 15 years = $500 times 15 years = $7500. Under Pereira W would get $7500 plus her $10,000 SP and the community would get the remaining $27,500.

Under the formula in Van Camp the community gets a reasonable salary for the value of the services of the owner spouse. The issue would be how much time did W devote to the business. Assuming a reasonable salary of $1,000 per year, the community would be entitled to $15,000 under this formula.

Pereira is applied where the community time and skill is the greater factor in the appreciation; Van Camp applies when business or economic factors produce the profits. Herb will argue that it was W's skill in managing the mutual fund that caused the appreciation. W will argue the market forces by themselves caused the increase. It would be up to the court to obtain more facts to determine who has the better argument.

The fact that title was taken in Wanda's name alone is not determinative. Form of title is not conclusive. Interest is the key. Title in one spouse's name alone is insufficient without more to overcome the general community property presumption. Wanda will argue that the oral agreement plus the fact of title in her own name alone should be sufficient for the courts to overcome the general community property presumption. This argument will fail due to the absence of a written, express declaration.

CALL 3. The Cabin

In 1995, H and W bought a vacation cabin in California for $75,000. They made a down payment of $25,000 with CP funds and took title as joint tenants. Facts also indicate that shortly after 1995 H inherited a large sum of money. As discussed, inherited funds are separate property. Therefore, when H used $50,000 of the inheritance to pay off the note, and another $20,000 of the inheritance to add a room, this $70,000 contribution was all H's SP.

Under the old rule in Lucas, when SP funds were used toward the purchase or improvement of property held in joint tenancy, the contribution was deemed a gift, absent an agreement to the contrary.

Under anti-Lucas legislation, the separate property is entitled to reimbursement, absent an agreement to the contrary. No facts indicate such an agreement. Therefore H will be entitled to reimbursement.

Under California CP law, property held in joint form, such as a joint tenancy, is presumed community property. Therefore, the $150,000 cabin will be presumed community property, but H will be entitled to $70,000 reimbursement. The community gets $80,000 and H gets $70,000.

Distribution

1. The $200,000 home
   H gets ½ of $176,000 plus $24,000.
   W gets ½ of $176,000.

2. The $45,000 Mutual Fund
   H gets ½; W gets ½ unless the court finds that the $10,000 is W's SP, when H will be entitled to something under the Pereira or Van Camp formulas.

3. The $150,000 Cabin
   H gets ½ of $80,000 plus $70,000.
   W gets ½ of $80,000.

[THIS PAGE INTENTIONALLY LEFT BLANK.]

Feb 2000

Question 1

H and W were married in 1985 in Franklin, a non-community property state. H worked as an engineer for Texco beginning in 1975. W worked as a bookkeeper. During his employment with Texco, H received annual bonuses in the form of Texco stock. By 1990, H owned 1.000 shares of Texco.

In 1990, H accepted a job offer from Calco, a California-based engineering firm, and H and W moved to California. In 1991, H and W purchased a condominium for $200,000, taking title as "H and W, husband and wife, as joint tenants with right of survivorship." W paid the $50,000 down payment with money she had recently inherited, and H and W obtained a $150,000 loan secured by a deed of trust for the balance of the purchase price. H made the monthly principal and interest payments o the loan out of his Calco earnings.

In 1999, W, who had found a bookkeeping job shortly after moving to California, was charged with embezzling $50,000 from that employer. W admitted spending the $50,000 on cocaine. W retained Lawyer, who negotiated a plea bargain pursuant to which W pled guilty, was placed on three years probation, and was ordered to make full restitution. W also underwent treatment at DrugStop, a drug treatment facility, at a cost of $10,000. Lawyer charged W $5,000 to handle the case.

H had no knowledge of either W's embezzlement or cocaine habit until her arrest. H has filed for dissolution of the marriage. The condominium is currently valued at $300,000 with a $50,000 balance on the mortgage.

What are H and W's respective rights and liabilities with regard to:

1. The 1,000 shares of Texco stock? Discuss.

2. The condominium? Discuss.

3. The attorney's fee, restitution, and expenses for the DrugStop treatment? Discuss.

Answer according to California law.

Use your key (attached) in analyzing this problem. A brief analysis follows.

CALL 1 – The Stock

H began accumulating the stock in 1975, 10 years before the marriage. He was married in 1985, and by 1990 had 1000 shares. The stock is quasi-community property. It was acquired by H in a non-community property state, but because it was a bonus for H's job skills it would have been considered community property if acquired in California.

At dissolution, QCP is treated as CP. The court will use the <u>time rule</u> to determine distribution. Using the time rule, the court will apportion to the community based on the ratio of years employed during the marriage divided by total number of years employed. The 1000 shares were acquired over 15 years, from 1975 – 1990. H and W were married for 5 of those 15 years (between 1985 and 1990). The community will be entitled to 5/15th (or 1/3) of the 1000 shares; H (SP) will be entitled to 10/15 or 2/3 of the 1000 shares.

CALL 2. The Condo

This is a Lucas/Anti-Lucas problem. Property is taken in joint tenancy form where there is a separate property contribution. Under Lucas the SP contribution was deemed a gift; under anti-Lucas legislation SP is entitled to reimbursement of any principal contribution (but not appreciation or interest). Thus, under anti-Lucas W will be entitled to reimbursement of her $50,000 but not to interest or appreciation.

Here, a $50,000 down payment was made with money W recently inherited. Inheritances are SP, so W's SP funds were used to make the down payment.

The loan was CP, because the court will look to the intent of the lender. Here, intent is clear because title was taken in joint tenancy form. The current value of the condo is $300,000. It has a $50,000 outstanding loan.

At dissolution, property in joint form will be presumed community property. Both the $300,000 condo and the $50,000 loan will be deemed community property.

Subtracting the $50,000 loan from the $300,000 value of the condo leaves $250,000. W will be entitled to $50,000 reimbursement, leaving $200,000 in CP funds and $50,000 in W's SP funds.

H gets ½ of $200,000; W gets ½ of $200,000 plus $50,000.

CALL 3.
Attorney Fees

Since 1975 spouses have equal rights of management and control. Either spouse may act alone and can deal with CP as his/her own, except for a CP business where the other spouse is the manager.

W contracted for attorney services during the marriage. She has a right to do this under the above rule. Further, CP is liable for debts acquired during the marriage. Because the attorney's $10,000 fee was acquired during the marriage, CP will be liable for the entire amount.

Restitution

CP is primarily liable for torts (or criminal fines/restitution) if the underlying conduct was for the benefit of the community. CP is secondarily liable if the underlying conduct was not for the benefit of the community.

Here, H had no knowledge of the embezzlement. More importantly, the $50,000 was not for the benefit of the community because it was spent on W's cocaine habit.

W's SP will be primarily liable for the restitution. If she does not have enough SP, then CP will be secondarily liable.

DrugStop

The SP of either spouse is liable for necessaries contracted during the marriage while the spouses are living together. If there is no SP, the CP is liable. Once W's SP is exhausted, H's SP or the CP will be liable because drug treatment is a medical necessity, and the treatment was contracted for, and completed, during the marriage.

COMMUNITY PROPERTY SCORING KEY-FEB 2000

PRESUMPTIONS...**5 pts.**

Community Property Rule: California is a community property state. This means that all property and debts acquired during the marriage is presumed to be community property.

Separate Property Rule: All property and debts acquired before marriage, after permanent separation, by gift, or by inheritance, including the rents, income, and profits thereof is separate property

CALL 1: THE 1,000 SHARES OF TEXCO STOCK. (35 points total)

Quasi-Community Property...**10 pts.**

Quasi-Community Property Rule: All property which is acquired by a married couple in another jurisdiction which would have been community property if the acquiring spouse was domiciled in California will be treated as community property at death or dissolution.

Background law: The source of quasi-community property remains separate property until death or dissolution, unless there is action by creditors. At death, if the non-owner spouse dies first, then the quasi-community property will remain separate property.

Use of facts: H & W were married in 1985 in Franklin, a non-community property state. H & W moved to California in 1990. Between 1985 and 1990, H worked as an engineer for Texco earning wages and also receiving annual bonuses in the form of Texco stock. During this time, W worked as a bookkeeper.

Conclusion: Once H & W move to California, the wages which each H & W earned and the stock which H earned during marriage will be considered quasi-community property.

Texco Stock...**25 pts.**

Background facts & law: H began working for Texco in 1975. During H's employment with Texco he received annual bonuses in the form of Texco stock, and by 1990 he owned 1,000 shares. H & W were married for five years of the fifteen year period in which H earned the Texco stock. The Texco stock was earned through H's time, skill, and effort. As such, the portion of the Texco stock which was earned during marriage is quasi-community property.

Time Rule: In order to determine the quasi-community property share of the Texco stock, it will be necessary to utilize the Time Rule which is determined by dividing the years employed during marriage by the total number of years employed.

Use of facts: Here H & W were married for one third of the time in which H was employed by Texco and earning Texco stock (5 years of marriage / 15 years employed at Texco).

Conclusion: Therefore 1/3 of the 1,000 shares of Texco stock is quasi-community property. Since H has filed for dissolution of marriage, this 1/3 portion of the Texco stock will be treated as community property to be divided equally between H & W. H will retain the remaining 2/3 of the Texco stock.

CALL 2: THE CONDO (30 points total)

Lucas..**10 pts.**

Background facts & law: In 1991, once H & W were living in California, H & W purchased a condominium for $200,000. H & W took title in the condo as "H and W, husband and wife, as joint tenants with the right of survivorship." W paid a $50,000 down payment with money she recently inherited. Such inheritance is W's separate property. The balance of the condo's purchase price was financed by a $150,000 loan which both H & W obtained. The monthly principal and interest payments on the loan was paid out of H's Calco earnings. These earnings are community property; hence community property is paying for the community property mortgage.

Lucas Rule: Prior to 1984, whenever a husband and wife in California took title in real property as "joint tenants," it was presumed that the use of separate property towards payment on the real property was a gift to the community. Hence, unless there was a written agreement otherwise, separate property funds paid toward the real property would not be reimbursed.

Conclusion: If Lucas were applied in this case, W would not be entitled to a reimbursement of the $50,000 separate property down payment toward the condo.

Anti-Lucas...**20 pts.**

Anti-Lucas Rule: After 1984, when a married couple took title in real property as "joint tenants," the property was presumed to be community property. Under Anti-Lucas, any separate property paid towards the community property asset would be reimbursed in the amount of the separate property contribution. However, the separate property will not share in the ownership of the property, meaning that the separate property will not be entitled to any share of the appreciation.

Background law: After 1987, the Anti-Lucas legislation was applied to all forms of title taken in joint and equal form, including tenants in common and tenants by the entirety.

Use of facts: Because H & W obtained the condo after 1984 and took title as "joint tenants with the right of survivorship," the Anti-Lucas Rule will apply. This means that the condo is presumed to be community property. Pursuant to the Anti-Lucas Rule, W will be entitled to a **reimbursement** of the $50,000 separate property down payment she made toward the condo. Unfortunately for W, the $50,000 separate property will not share in the $300,000 appreciation value of the condo. However, the community will receive a **pro-rata share** in the $300,000 appreciation of the condo.

Conclusion: After subtracting W's $50,000 separate property share from the $300,000 value of the home, the community is left with a $250,000 share in the condo. There still is a $50,000 balance on the mortgage, and since the mortgage was obtained by both H & W, it is a community property debt. After paying off the balance on the mortgage, there is $200,000 left in the condo which will be distributed equally between H & W.

CALL 3: (30 points total)
ATTORNEY'S FEES...**10 pts.**

Background law: Spouses have equal management and control over community property. As such, each spouse may make purchases or assume debts on behalf of the community.

Use of facts: W retained Lawyer to represent her after she was charged with embezzling $50,000 from her employer. Lawyer charged W $5,000 to handle her case. Since both H & W have equal management powers over the community property, the community will be liable for the $5,000 debt to Lawyer. W's separate property will also be liable for the attorney fees. However, unless the court characterizes Lawyer's fees as "necessaries," then H's separate property will not be liable for the $5,000 in attorney fees.

Conclusion: Upon dissolution, the court may decide to distribute the debt to Lawyer to W, unless the interests of justice would provide otherwise. Nonetheless, the community will still be liable for the $5,000 to Lawyer.

RESTITUTION...**10 pts.**

Background law: The community may be liable for torts of either spouse. If the tort was committed for the benefit of the community, then the community is primarily liable for the tort. But, if the tort was not committed for the benefit of the community, then the separate property of the spouse who committed the tort will be primarily liable and the community will be secondarily liable.

Use of facts: W was charged with embezzling $50,000 from her employer and W admitted to spending the $50,000 on cocaine. H had no knowledge of either W's embezzlement or cocaine habit until W was arrested. W spent the $50,000 she embezzled entirely on herself and did not use any of the money to benefit the community.

Conclusion: W's separate property will be primarily liable to pay $50,000 in restitution. The community will be secondarily liable if W's separate property is not sufficient to cover the full amount of the restitution. H's separate property will not be liable for any of the restitution.

EXPENSES FOR THE DRUGSTOP TREATMENT...**10 pts.**

Background law: The separate property of either spouse is liable for necessaries contracted by the other spouse while living together (i.e. medical expenses).

Use of facts: W underwent treatment at a drug treatment facility at a cost of $10,000. This treatment occurred while H & W were still married and living together. W's treatment can be argued to be a necessary medical expense.

Conclusion: Therefore, both H's separate property and the community property, as well as W's separate property, will be liable for the $10,000 spent for W's DrugStop treatment.

[THIS PAGE INTENTIONALLY LEFT BLANK.]

Feb 1999

Question 3

On July 1, 1991, Hank ("H") and Wanda ("W") married in Illinois, a non-community property state. W began law school in August 1991, and graduated in June 1994. During this period, H worked as a stockbroker and earned a graduate degree in art history. Of W's $60,000 in law school tuition, $50,000 was paid with an education loan obtained by H from Bank. The remaining $10,000 was paid with H's wages, as were H's $15,000 tuition and W's $40,000 in living expenses while attending law school.

H and W moved to California in 1994. W began work as an associate in a law firm, and H continued to work as a stockbroker. In 1996, H bought a Ming vase with his wages and gave it to W on her birthday. At W's suggestion, H bought a Chinese-style table for their living room, on which to display the vase. They both frequently referred to the vase as "our pride and joy."

In July 1998, H and W separated and filed for dissolution of their marriage. At the time, the balance due on the education loan was $10,000. On December 31, 1998, W received a substantial year-end bonus from her firm. A judgment of dissolution was entered in January 1999.

In the distribution of property and allocation of liabilities of H and W, how should the court treat:

1. W's legal education and law degree? Discuss.

2. The $10,000 balance on the education loan? Discuss.

3. H's art history degree? Discuss.

4. The vase? Discuss.

5. The bonus? Discuss.

Answer according to California law.

CALL 1 – W's Legal Education and Law Degree

California is a community property state. All property and debts acquired during the marriage is presumed to be <u>community property</u> (CP) and will be treated as such absent an express declaration to the contrary, clear and convincing evidence to the contrary, or an exception created by case law or by statute.

<u>Quasi Community Property</u> (QCP) is property (wherever situated) acquired by a married couple in another jurisdiction that would have been CP if the acquiring spouse was domiciled in California. QCP remains the SP of the acquiring spouse except at death, dissolution, and in an action by creditors.

H and W were married on July 1, 1991 in Illinois, a non-CP state. They moved to California in 1994. Hence, any property H and W acquired between July 1, 1991 and 1994 is QCP. Because the marriage was dissolved in January 1999, such property will be treated as community property.

In August 1991 W went to law school, and she graduated in June of 1994. It appears as though the couple then moved to California that same year where W began working as an associate attorney.

The issue is whether the legal education and law degree, acquired in Illinois, would have been community property if acquired in California. The California Supreme Court, in interpreting relevant legislative enactments has ruled that a professional education, license, degree, or training does not constitute community property. This is because a professional education/degree is not encompassed within the concept of property. It has no exchange value and terminates with the death of the holder. Therefore, the legal education and law degree will be treated by the court as W's separate property.

<u>Reimbursement</u>

The next issue is whether the community is entitled to reimbursement. W had $60,000 in law school tuition paid for by a $50,000 loan obtained by H from bank plus $10,000 of H's wages. She also had $40,000 in living expenses paid for by H's wages.

The fact that H took out the loan is of little consequence. Courts look to the intent of the lender. Here, the loan was for W's education, so the lender no doubt intended to hold both H and W responsible for the loan. Thus, the loan, having been acquired while the couple was domiciled in Illinois, is a QCP debt and will be treated as a CP.

The community will be entitled to reimbursement from W for any community funds that went toward repayment of the loan. The rule in California is, absent an express agreement to the contrary, the community is entitled to reimbursement for community contributions to education or training that substantially enhance the educated party's earning capacity.

H will have no trouble arguing that obtaining a law degree enhanced W's earning capacity, so the community will be entitled to reimbursement. However, the courts have held that reimbursement is limited to educational expenses (books, tuition, etc.). Case law in California has specifically excluded living expenses. Therefore the community will be entitled to reimbursement of the $40,000 of the $50,000 loan that was paid off during the existence of the community. The community will not be entitled to reimbursement for the community funds (H's wages while married) that were used for W's living expenses.

W's Defense and the 10 Year Rule

The California courts have further held that the community is not entitled to reimbursement if the community has benefited from the educated spouse's education. There is a presumption that after 10 years the community has so benefited and is therefore not entitled to reimbursement.

This defense will fail. W graduated in June of 1994. The marriage dissolved in January of 1999, after less than 5 years. W will have the burden of overcoming the presumption by clear and convincing evidence, and no facts indicate she will succeed.

Call 2. The $10,000 Balance on the Loan

The legislature has passed a clear rule (§ 2641) governing loans incurred during marriage for education. The loan is assigned to the educated spouse at dissolution, and becomes the SP of the educated spouse.

Presently, there is a $10,000 balance on W's education loan. The court will assign this debt to W as her SP.

Call 3. H's Art History Degree

The rule discussed earlier is that the degree remains H's SP. Whether the community is entitled to reimbursement will hinge on whether H's art degree substantially enhanced his earning capacity.

The facts indicate that H used his wages to pay $15,000 in tuition for his art degree. Because these wages were acquired during the existence of the community they are QCP and will be treated as CP at dissolution. Thus, CP funds were used to pay H's tuition.

Facts further stipulate that H worked as a stockbroker while he earned the degree. He continued to work as a stockbroker even after obtaining the degree. H will argue that the art degree did not enhance his earning capacity, and therefore the community is not entitled to reimbursement. This is a close call.

Although H has not yet used his degree, it cannot be denied that this degree may have enhanced his future earning potential. Further, the court can consider this degree in evaluating spousal support. It is not an element of spousal support. Such support is determined on the basis of need. However, it is unlikely that the court will force W to reimburse the community and let H benefit from his degree without reimbursement. In all likelihood, the court will order H to reimburse. The standard is "in the interests of justice and equity."

Call 4. The Vase

H bought a Ming vase with wages acquired during the community. Therefore the vase was acquired with CP funds. The issue is whether his gift transmuted the CP to W's SP.

Transmutation/Gift

In California, property rights may be altered (transmuted) by agreement. This applies generally (*e.g.*, CP to SP; SP to CP, etc.). No consideration is needed. Prior to 1985, oral agreements proved by conduct generally prevailed; no formal requirements were enforced. From 1985 to the present, such agreements must be in writing by express declaration. Facts do not indicate a writing.

There is an exception for gifts. As of July 1987 California courts require a writing unless the gift is of a personal nature and not substantial in value given the marriage.

The vase was purchased in 1996 and given to W by H at that time. There was no writing. The vase was not of a personal nature; the couple put it on display and referred to it (and the table H bought at W's suggestion) as "our pride and joy." Further, it is unlikely that such a vase is not substantial in value given the marriage. H and W are not wealthy. In fact, they appear to be in some debt. Therefore, a writing will be required. As none exists, the vase will be held to be a CP asset.

Call 5. The Bonus

Separate Property and Separation

Separate property is all property acquired before marriage, after permanent separation, by gift or inheritance and all profits therefrom.

W obtained a substantial bonus on Dec. 31, 1998, about 6 months after separation. Thus, W will argue that the bonus is SP.

Time Rule

H will counter that the bonus was for work completed during the entire year, and was a reward for her skill and labor. As such, a portion of the bonus is community property.

In such circumstances, the court will apply the time rule. The community will be entitled to a pro rata share of the asset. Assuming that H and W were separated for 6 months and married for the other 6 months of the year when W got the bonus, the community will be entitled to ½ of the bonus. The remaining ½ will be W's SP. Thus, H will get ¼ and W ¾ of the bonus.

[THIS PAGE INTENTIONALLY LEFT BLANK.]

In 1974, Hugh (H), a resident of Iowa, a non-community property state, began working there for Apex. Apex has an employee retirement plan which gives to each employee who retires after 20 years of continuous employment with the company the option of receiving either a lifetime monthly pension payment or an actuarially equivalent single lump sum payment. H eventually retired from Apex in 1994.

In 1997, H obtained a credit card which carried with it, free of extra charge, a $200,000 travel accident life insurance benefit on each commercial aviation flight ticket purchased with the credit card. The annual charge for the credit card was paid each year by H from his Apex salary and, after his retirement in 1994, from wages of a part-time job he held.

In 1983, H married Wendy (W) in Iowa, and H and W went to California on their honeymoon. While there, they visited a television studio where W appeared on a quiz show and won a condominium in California worth $100,000. W took title to the condominium in her name alone. After their return to Iowa, H and W decided to move to California and live in the condominium. Apex had offices in California, and H arranged to be transferred there. H and W moved into the condominium in 1984.

In 1990, H received a sizeable bonus from Apex in recognition of his extraordinary work for the firm in 1989. Unknown to W, H used the bonus as a down payment on the purchase of an office building in California, taking title in his name alone. In November 1994, he sold the building for a small profit to a purchaser who paid full value and who was aware that H was married. The building has since increased substantially in value because of the announcement of the construction of a new shopping center nearby.

When H retired from Apex in 1994, he chose the lump sum payment option available under his retirement plan and received $200,000 in cash which he used to buy U.S. Savings Bonds. He had the bonds registered, "H, Pay on Death to George." Under the applicable federal statute, such designation means that H is owner of the bond, but it is "payable on death" of H to George (G), who is H's brother.

In January 1995, H was killed on a flight to visit G. The credit card company's insurance carrier paid $200,000 to H's estate. H's will confirmed to W her interest in their community and quasi-community property and gave all property over which he had power of testamentary disposition to G.

What are the rights of W and G to each of the following properties?

1. The condominium? Discuss.

2. The office building? Discuss.

3. The bonds? Discuss.

4. The life insurance proceeds? Discuss.

Answer according to California law.

CALL 1 – The Condo

Begin by defining CP, SP, and QCP. Be sure to note that QCP remains the SP of the acquiring spouse except at death, dissolution, or action by creditors. Further note that if the non-acquiring spouse dies first, the QCP remains the SP of the acquiring spouse.

QCP is a big issue because H and W were married in Iowa, a non-CP state, in 1983. While on a visit to California they won a condo worth $100,000. W took title in her name alone. All this occurred while H and W were residents of Iowa. Had the couple been married in California at the time, the fact that W took title in her name alone would not control; interest is controlling. The property was obtained while they were married, so its source would have been CP. The issue would then be transmutation or gift. Because this occurred in 1983, under California law W would have probably prevailed in her claim that H gave her a gift or that this was a transmutation of CP to W's SP. Had this occurred after July 1987, W would have needed an express declaration for the transmutation (effective Jan. 1, 1985) or gift (effective July 1, 1987).

However, because the condo was QCP at the time of acquisition, it remained as such until H was killed on a flight to visit George. As QCP the condo would have remained W's QCP. Note, however, that one of the sample answers provided by the Bar failed to address the issue of whether the condo would have been CP had it been acquired in California. As indicated, it would have been; but because this took place before 1985 W would have prevailed on either a gift or transmutation theory (given that title was in her name alone). Also notice that the Bar's sample answer B does a good job of arguing in the alternative on distribution.

CALL 2 – The Office Building

This is the second time the Bar has given us facts about a sleaze spouse who acquired property with CP funds, took title in his name alone, and transferred the property without the other spouse's knowledge or consent.

The relevant law can be found in the schema under third party transfers. The general rule is equal right to management and control. However, you should note it is a breach of a fiduciary duty for one spouse to sell CP real property without the other spouse's knowledge and consent.

In 1990 H received a sizable bonus. The bonus is CP because it was acquired during the marriage by H's skill and labor (extraordinary work). Without W's consent, H purchased real property and then sold it to a purchaser who knew he was married.

There are two important points. First, H's taking title in his name alone is not conclusive; interest is the key, and the building is CP because CP funds and CP effort went into its acquisition. Second, and perhaps even more important, the purchaser was <u>not</u> a BFP because he knew of the marriage.

Facts indicate the building was sold in Nov. 1994 and H was killed in Jan. 1995. Therefore the transaction falls within the 1-year statute of limitations. The law is that if W had discovered a sale to a <u>BFP</u> before H's death, she could set aside the whole transaction with reimbursement for the BFP.

After H's death she would only be allowed to set aside ½. However, because the purchaser is <u>not</u> a BFP W can set the entire transaction aside (with reimbursement).

The law further holds that spouses can will away their ½ of the CP and all of their SP. H's will confirmed W's interest in the community and quasi-community property, but he may will away his own CP interests. Therefore, if the deal is set aside, W will get ½ and George will get ½.

CALL 3 -- The Bonds

The issue is Federal Preemption. Federal law preempts California CP laws because of the Supremacy Clause. The exception is fraud. When H purchased the bonds using his retirement money, he was defrauding W out of her rightful CP share. Federal law will not apply, and the courts will calculate W's CP share.

The courts will use the <u>time rule</u>. H worked for 20 years (1974 – 1994). Of those 20 years, he was married 11 (1983 – 1994). Therefore, 9/20 of the bonds is H's SP, which he can will to G. 11/20 are CP. Of the 11/20, ½ will go to W and ½ to G.

CALL 4 --The Wife's Insurance Proceeds

Where term insurance is involved, the source of funds for the policy are those that were used at the beginning of each year because term insurance is year-to-year. H paid for the policy through the annual charges to his credit card. He used his salary and after 1994 wages from a part-time job. Because the funds for the <u>last</u> annual payment were CP, having been acquired by H's effort during the marriage, the proceeds from the policy will be considered CP. Therefore W will get half and G the other half.

If you have time, you can make an argument to apportion according to the time rule because H first obtained the policy in 1977, five years before his marriage. Therefore, 5 of the 18 years he held the policy were SP. This argument will fail, however, for the reasons given above.

[THIS PAGE INTENTIONALLY LEFT BLANK.]

[THIS PAGE INTENTIONALLY LEFT BLANK.]